Buddhism for Beginners

12 Life-Changing Practices for Modern Everyday Life—Easy Ways to Reduce Stress, Clear Your Mind, and Achieve Inner Peace

Sophia Shell

Table of Contents

An Introduction to Buddhism

I have a question for you. Have you ever felt like stress is that guest who shows up uninvited and then just won't leave? In 2024, a whopping 75% of Americans had that same guest show up, reporting dealing with physical or mental stress (SingleCare Team, 2024). If you've ever wrestled with anxiety, caught yourself spiraling in overthinking, or felt completely burned out, you're in good company. Now, imagine meeting life's challenges with a clear mind, a light heart, and a sense of calm. That's where Buddhism can step in as your gentle guide.

Buddhism isn't some far-off relic of ancient Eastern traditions—it's a warm, inviting way of living that brings balance and peace into your everyday world. Over 2,500 years ago, a prince named Siddhartha Gautama traded his royal comforts for a quest to understand human suffering. Through deep meditation and honest self-reflection, he found a path to enlightenment and earned the name "the Buddha," or the Awakened One (History.com Editors, 2024).

At its heart, Buddhism invites you to simply observe your thoughts and emotions without harsh judgment. It hands you practical tools to handle the messy, unpredictable moments of life—without insisting on one right way to do things. Maybe you're looking to add a dash of mindfulness to your daily routine, or perhaps you're craving a complete shift in perspective. Maybe you're looking for calm instead of chaos. I mean, who isn't? I want you to know that this process, this journey, is personal, adaptable, and totally achievable. And hey, you won't need to climb any mountains or shave your head to get started! Unless that's your thing—and in that case, go for it!

This book gently invites you to explore 12 transformative practices inspired by Buddhist wisdom. Each practice is thoughtfully crafted to be accessible, practical, and truly life-changing, guiding you toward reduced stress, a clearer mind, and a deeper sense of inner peace. Whether you're handling the demands of a busy professional life, a student balancing various challenges, or anyone seeking a more serene and meaningful existence, these nurturing principles are here to support you on your journey.

Within this book, you'll discover

- an understanding of the core principles of Buddhism in a simple, relatable way.

- a tool kit of achievable daily habits and rituals to create mindfulness and peace.

- how to gain confidence in applying Buddhist wisdom to real-life challenges—without feeling overwhelmed.

- a complete a four-week practice plan to integrate these life-changing habits into your routine.

Each chapter introduces a Buddhist principle and a practical way to integrate it into your daily life. These practices aren't about perfection—they're about progress.

This isn't about adding more to your already busy life. It's about making simple shifts in the way you think, react, and approach each day. Even small, consistent changes can lead to amazing changes.

So, let's take a deep breath together. You don't need to be perfect. You don't need to have it all figured out. You just need an open mind and a willingness to explore.

Let's begin.

Chapter 1:
Understanding Life Challenges (Dukkha)

Imagine you've had one of those days. You wake up late, spill coffee on your shirt, get stuck in traffic, and then receive a text with bad news. It's enough to make you want to crawl back into bed and start over. Or maybe your challenges run deeper—grief, loneliness, self-doubt, or the nagging feeling that something's missing, even when life looks fine from the outside.

Welcome to *dukkha*, the First Noble Truth—a central concept in Buddhism, often translated as suffering, dissatisfaction, or, simply, the struggles of being human (Huxter, n.d.-a). But before you imagine a bleak philosophy of doom and gloom, know this: Buddhism doesn't dwell on suffering to make life feel heavier. Instead, it teaches us to see it clearly, understand it, and, most importantly, free ourselves from its grip.

Dukkha isn't just the big, painful moments of loss or hardship. It's also the everyday frustrations, the discomfort of wanting things to be different, and even the stress of trying to hold on to happiness, fearing it will slip away. It's the common thread that connects us all—because no one escapes life without facing challenges. The good news? Understanding *dukkha* is the first step to finding peace within it.

This chapter will explore why suffering is an inevitable part of life but also why it doesn't have to define us. We'll look at how we resist discomfort, how that resistance actually deepens our struggles, and how shifting our perspective can change everything. By learning to meet life's challenges with awareness and acceptance, we can loosen suffering's grip and respond with more wisdom, ease, and even—dare I say—freedom.

There's no perfect way to practice this and no rush to fix anything. I'm not trying to share Buddhism with you in an attempt to escape suffering. Instead, Buddhism offers a gentle path, one step at a time, toward a lighter and more peaceful way of living.

Throughout this chapter, and the book, you'll notice the word suffering comes up a lot—it's a key term in Buddhism. But I want to pause here and make sure we're on the same page about what it really means.

When Buddhists talk about suffering, they're not only referring to life's big, heartbreaking moments, like grief, illness, or loss. Suffering also includes the smaller, everyday struggles—the moments that leave us feeling uncomfortable, stressed, or stuck. In simple terms, it's any kind of negative feeling, discomfort, doubt, or emotional struggle you face.

So, when you see "suffering" used in this book, think of it as a broad term covering everything from life's deep pain to those everyday annoyances that can weigh on us. It could be

- the frustration of sitting in traffic when you're already late.

- the anxiety that creeps in before an important meeting or social event.

- the loneliness you feel when you're scrolling through social media, wondering if everyone else has life figured out.

- the self-doubt that tells you you're not doing enough or being enough.

- the heartbreak from a relationship that didn't work out the way you'd hoped.

Buddhism doesn't ignore these struggles or ask you to pretend they don't exist. Instead, it offers gentle, practical ways to understand them, work through them, and, over time, experience less of that suffering—or at least relate to it differently.

Acknowledging Suffering Without Judgment

Recognizing suffering in our lives is a crucial step toward healing and personal growth. However, it's essential to approach this recognition without blame or judgment. Embracing our vulnerabilities allows us to connect with our shared humanity and fosters empathy toward ourselves and others.

Recognizing the Universality of Suffering

Suffering is an inherent part of the human experience; it's something that all of us encounter in various forms throughout our lives. It can look like relationships ending, losing a job, or daily frustrations and anxiety, as mentioned above. By acknowledging that everyone goes through their own struggles, we begin to see that we're not alone in our pain. This realization helps dismantle feelings of isolation and creates a sense of connection with others.

Understanding that suffering exists universally among us paves the way for empathy, allowing us to be more compassionate toward ourselves and those around us. When we recognize that our challenges are part of a common thread of existence, we take the first step toward healing—for ourselves, and for the collective human experience.

Identifying Suffering in Daily Life

So, how do we become aware of suffering in our everyday lives? First, it's important to practice mindfulness and observe discomforts without an immediate reaction. This means taking a moment to acknowledge physical, emotional, or psychological discomfort when it arises, without acting on the urge to push it away or judge ourselves for feeling it.

Here are some practical strategies to gently observe suffering in your routines:

- **Mindful observation:** Set aside a few moments each day for mindful observation. Whether you're feeling stressed, anxious, or physically unwell, pause to acknowledge what you're experiencing. Instead of condemning these feelings, ask yourself what they might be teaching you.

- **Journaling:** Keep a journal to note instances of suffering you encounter. For example, maybe you're struggling with some new anxiety because of a relationship coming to an end. Writing can help you clarify your feelings and understand how they fit into the larger picture of your life. Reflecting on these experiences can show patterns and areas where you can grow.

- **Breathing exercises:** Try simple breathing exercises when discomfort arises. Inhale deeply and acknowledge the sensation of suffering; then exhale slowly, releasing the judgment tied to it. This practice allows you to feel your emotions without becoming overwhelmed.

- **Compassionate self-talk:** When you notice suffering, speak to yourself with kindness. Remind yourself that it's okay to feel this way and that you're part of a larger community of beings who experience the same challenges.

When you cultivate these practices, you can develop a more compassionate relationship with your suffering, allowing it to guide you toward healing rather than holding you captive. Remember that acknowledging suffering without judgment is a practice and a pathway toward deeper understanding and connection with yourself and others.

Cultivating Self-Compassion

In moments of suffering, it's easy to fall into the trap of harsh self-criticism. We often think we should be stronger, braver, or more resilient. But embracing ourselves during these challenging times is a powerful act of kindness. Understanding and practicing self-compassion can significantly alleviate the weight of suffering, providing us with the emotional support we truly need.

Embracing Yourself Without Harsh Self-Criticism

Self-compassion means treating yourself with the same kindness and understanding you'd offer to a dear friend facing similar challenges. When you experience suffering, it's vital to use compassionate language when speaking to yourself. Instead of saying, "I shouldn't feel this way," try reframing your self-talk to something like, "It's okay to feel this way. I'm doing my best."

Here are some tips to cultivate self-compassion during tough times:

- **Pause and acknowledge:** When you feel suffering surface, take a moment to pause and acknowledge your feelings without judgment. Recognize that it's okay to be where you are.

- **Use gentle language:** Monitor your inner dialogue. Swap out critical remarks for supportive words. Instead of saying, "I'm such a failure," say, "I'm experiencing a tough moment, and that's okay."

- **Write a letter to yourself:** Imagine you're writing to a friend going through the same struggle. What would you say to comfort and support them? Write that down as a letter to yourself.

- **Practice forgiveness:** Understand that everyone has flaws and makes mistakes—yourself included. Allow yourself to forgive your perceived shortcomings, just as you would for others.

The Role of Mindfulness in Acknowledgment

Mindfulness can be an incredible tool for recognizing suffering. It invites us to observe our experiences without judgment, offering a clearer lens through which we can understand our feelings. When practiced regularly, mindfulness creates a space for healing and understanding, allowing us to address suffering without immediately reacting to it.

Here are some unique mindfulness exercises to help you observe suffering in real time:

- **Body scan:** Find a comfortable position, close your eyes, and take deep breaths. Slowly bring your awareness to different areas of your body, noticing any tension or discomfort. Acknowledge these sensations without trying to change them, creating a compassionate awareness of your physical state.

- **Mindful listening:** Choose a sound in your environment—like chirping birds or the hum of a fan. Focus solely on that sound, allowing your thoughts to drift as you listen. This practice can pull you into the present moment, reminding you to recognize and accept your feelings without judgment.

- **Five senses exercise:** Take a moment to engage each of your five senses. Identify one thing you can see, hear, touch, taste, and smell. This practice grounds you in the present and encourages observation without emotional reaction, helping you clarify your feelings of suffering.

- **Compassionate breathing:** As you breathe in, silently say to yourself, "In this moment, I accept my suffering." As you breathe out, say, "I release judgment." This exercise helps to cultivate a nonjudgmental approach to your experiences.

Choosing to integrate these practices into your daily life allows you to develop a nurturing relationship with yourself and the ability to acknowledge suffering with compassion. Remember, embracing self-compassion is a journey that, over time, leads to deeper healing and a greater sense of connection with yourself and the world around you.

Insights From Mindful Observation of Discomfort

Mindful observation of our discomforts opens the door to valuable insights about the nature of our suffering, enabling personal growth. By gently observing our experiences without judgment, we can uncover layers of emotion and thought that contribute to our discomfort, ultimately leading to deeper understanding and transformation.

Understanding the Layers of Suffering

Mindful observation allows us to explore the roots and impacts of our discomfort more profoundly. When we intentionally observe our suffering, we can reveal emotions and thoughts that may be hidden beneath the surface. This exploration encourages us to differentiate between surface-level discomfort—such as stress or anxiety—and deeper issues that might be causing those sensations. Let's look at an example.

Imagine you're stuck in traffic, running late for work. Your initial reaction is clear—stress and impatience. But if you pause and mindfully observe, you might notice deeper layers:

- **Surface-level discomfort:** "I'm so annoyed! I hate being late!"

- **Deeper layer:** "I'm worried my boss will think I'm irresponsible."

- **Root issue:** A deeper fear of being seen as incompetent or letting people down.

When you take note of these layers, you're not simply stuck in traffic anymore. You're understanding how much of your stress comes not just from the situation but from the stories and fears running in the background.

This awareness can lead to meaningful change as you begin to manage your emotional landscape with more clarity.

Physical Sensations and Emotional Responses

One important aspect of mindful observation is recognizing how physical sensations correlate with emotional responses. For example, tension in the shoulders might accompany feelings of anxiety, while a heavy feeling in the chest might signal sadness. When we become attuned to our bodily sensations, we can better connect them with our emotional states.

To help you with this connection, consider these tools:

- **Body mapping:** Spend some time sitting quietly and bringing awareness to different parts of your body. Notice where you feel tension or discomfort, then reflect on any emotions associated with that area. Are there feelings that seem to arise in the same space?

- **Journal your experience:** Keep a journal where you jot down any physical sensations you notice throughout the day alongside the emotions you're feeling. Over time, you may begin to see patterns that connect certain emotions to specific physical experiences.

- **Practice mindful movement:** Engage in gentle activities like yoga or stretching that encourage you to pay attention to how your body feels while moving. Notice any emotional states that arise during or after your movements.

Using Observation as a Tool for Insight

Mindful observation serves as a powerful tool for gaining clarity in our understanding of suffering. By observing discomfort without immediate intervention, we create space for acceptance and understanding, transforming suffering into an opportunity for personal growth.

When we allow ourselves to simply be with our discomfort, we can glean insight from the experience. Ask yourself questions such as: "What is this discomfort teaching me? How does it influence my thoughts or actions?" This process can lead to healing as we uncover new perspectives on our experiences.

Harnessing Mindfulness Practices for Insight

To cultivate mindfulness in observing discomfort effectively, consider these practices:

- **Mindful breathing:** Take a few moments each day to focus solely on your breath. As you breathe in and out, observe any discomfort that arises without reacting. This practice helps you develop awareness of your sensations.

- **Three-minute breathing space:** When faced with discomfort, take three minutes to connect with your breath and observe how you feel. Spend the first minute noticing your physical sensations, the second minute observing your emotions, and the last minute reflecting on any insights gained from this practice.

- **Curiosity journaling:** After practicing mindful observation, journal about what you've noticed. Approach discomfort with curiosity instead of aversion. Consider writing down these questions and trying to answer them: "What is this discomfort trying to tell me?" or "How can this experience facilitate my growth?"

I encourage you to approach discomfort with curiosity rather than avoidance. This can change your relationship with suffering. When you embrace these mindfulness practices, you can gain valuable insights into the nature of your discomfort and begin a journey of personal growth and self-discovery. Remember, each moment of suffering can be a stepping stone toward greater understanding and transformation in your life.

Final Thoughts

As we move through our understanding of suffering, self-compassion, and mindful observation, we discover that awareness is our greatest ally. Embracing our discomfort with kindness and curiosity lets us unearth profound insights, shows us our struggles, and paves the way for personal growth and healing. Each layer of suffering we uncover provides an opportunity for change, reminding us that our experiences aren't just burdens to bear but essential elements of our shared humanity.

With this newfound perspective, you're now better equipped to approach challenges with compassion and mindfulness. The habits you build and the insights you gain can empower you to handle the complexities of your emotional landscape with grace and understanding.

As we move to the next chapter, we'll explore the concept of craving and how it can subtly govern our lives. This discussion will explore the nature of cravings, their role in our suffering, and how recognizing and changing these desires can lead to profound freedom. Prepare to uncover how letting go of excessive wanting can show you a path to inner peace and contentment.

Chapter 2:

Trapped by Wanting—How Craving Rules Our Lives (Samudaya)

You know that feeling when you finally get something you've been wanting—a new phone, a better job, a compliment from someone you admire—and, for a moment, everything feels just right? It's like a little hit of happiness, a spark of "Yes! This is what I needed." But then, before you know it, the glow fades. You start thinking about the next thing. Maybe the phone isn't as fast as you thought it would be. Maybe the job comes with stress you didn't expect. Maybe the compliment isn't quite enough. So, the cycle starts again: wanting, getting, feeling satisfied for a moment, then wanting more.

Buddhism has a name for this loop: *samudaya*, the truth of craving. It's the second of the Four Noble Truths, and it teaches us that so much of our stress, dissatisfaction, and suffering comes from one simple (but tricky) thing: wanting things to be different from how they are (Oakes, 2018).

We chase what we think will make us happy—a better body, more money, a perfect relationship—believing that once we have it, we'll feel content. And yet, somehow, there's always something else. If we're not craving something we don't have, we're clinging to what we do have, afraid to lose it. We crave pleasure, avoid discomfort, and get stuck in a tug-of-war between what we think we need and what life actually gives us. No wonder we feel exhausted.

When we recognize this cycle, we can start freeing ourselves from it. This chapter is about understanding how craving sneaks into our lives, why it leaves us feeling restless, and how Buddhist practices can help us step off the hamster wheel of wanting.

You don't have to give up all desires and live in a cave to find peace. It's not about rejecting joy, love, or ambition. It's about seeing our cravings for what they are—passing clouds, not the sky itself. And when we learn to loosen our grip on them, life starts to feel a whole lot lighter.

Let's explore how.

Reflecting on Personal Desires and Their Impacts

Have you ever convinced yourself that you needed something—really, truly needed it—only to get it and feel... underwhelmed? Maybe it was a new car, a dream vacation, or even the approval of someone whose opinion you valued. For a while, it felt like the missing piece. But then, like clockwork, a new craving appeared—and suddenly, you were back in the chase, believing that this next thing would be the one to finally make you feel complete.

It's not just you. It's human nature.

Desire, at its core, isn't the enemy. It's what gets us out of bed in the morning, fuels our passions, and pushes us to grow. But when desire takes the wheel, dictating our happiness, it can feel like we're always reaching and never arriving. And that can be exhausting.

Let's take a moment to reflect on how our personal desires influence our mental well-being and contribute to stress—because when we see desire clearly, we can shift our relationship with it in a way that brings more peace, not less joy.

Understanding Desire: The Longing That Never Ends

Desires can be tricky. They whisper, "Once you have this, you'll finally be happy." But what they don't tell us is that they're insatiable. The moment one desire is met, another appears. It's like trying to fill a bucket with a hole in the bottom—it never feels quite full.

When we pin our happiness on something outside of ourselves—more money, a bigger house, fancier clothes—we give desire the power to keep us perpetually dissatisfied. The key isn't to reject our desires or pretend we don't have them because, let's be honest, that won't work. Instead, we can acknowledge them without being ruled by them.

Why not give this a try: The next time you catch yourself *really* wanting something, pause for a second. Notice what it feels like in your body. Where do you feel it? Is it in your chest? Your stomach? Then, ask yourself, "Do I really need this, or is this just a momentary craving?" Most of the time, you'll realize the urgency isn't real—it's just a passing wave.

And if the desire remains? That's okay, too. Simply recognizing its nature—fleeting, never fully satisfied—helps loosen its grip.

Impact on Relationships: The Weight of Expectations

Desires don't just affect our personal happiness—they shape our relationships, too.

Think about the expectations you place on others: "I wish they would text me first for once." "If they really cared, they'd just know what I need." "They should be more ambitious, more relaxed, more affectionate, more like I want them to be."

When we cling too tightly to how we think others should be, we set ourselves up for frustration. No one—no matter how much they love us—can meet all of our expectations all of the time. And when we measure relationships by how well they align with our desires, we miss the beauty of what's actually there.

A small shift can make a huge difference: Instead of expecting, try observing. The next time you feel disappointed by someone, ask yourself, "Was I expecting something from them that they never actually agreed to give?" This little question can turn resentment into understanding, allowing relationships to breathe instead of suffocating under the weight of unchecked expectations.

Desire and Stress: When the Chase Steals Our Peace

Now, let's talk about stress.

Desires have a way of keeping us stuck in the future—chasing, planning, worrying. We tell ourselves we'll be happy *when*—when we lose the weight, when we land the promotion, when we find the right person. But this kind of thinking tricks us into postponing happiness indefinitely.

Ironically, the more we chase, the more restless we become. Even when we achieve a goal, we're often too busy thinking about the next one to fully enjoy it.

A powerful practice to counter this? A "What Actually Matters" list. At the end of each day, before bed, write down three things that truly mattered that day—not things you achieved, but moments that brought real meaning. Maybe it was a deep conversation. Maybe it was the way the sunlight hit the trees while you were driving. Maybe it was a moment of quiet peace with your pet.

The more you focus on what actually brings you joy in real time, the less power unfulfilled desires have over you.

Changing Perspective: From Craving to Contentment

The good news? We don't have to eliminate desire to find peace— we just have to change how we relate to it.

Instead of fighting against what we want or convincing ourselves we shouldn't have desires, we can practice acceptance—accepting that desires come and go, but they don't have to control us.

Here's a simple way to practice:

1. Notice the desire when it arises. No judgment, just awareness.

2. Acknowledge it as part of being human. "Ah, there's that craving again."

3. Shift focus to the present. Instead of letting the desire dictate your mood, take a deep breath and look around. What in this moment is already enough?

The more you practice contentment, the more you realize that peace isn't found in finally getting everything you want—it's found in making peace with what you already have.

And that? That changes everything.

Practicing Nonattachment Through Contemplation

Letting go isn't easy. Whether it's a dream we've been holding onto, a relationship we've poured our heart into, or even a stubborn idea of how things should be, loosening our grip can feel uncomfortable—even scary.

But nonattachment doesn't mean we stop caring. It just means we stop clinging.

It's the difference between holding a butterfly gently in an open palm and gripping it so tightly it can't fly. When we cling too tightly—whether to people, possessions, or even our own ideas—we create suffering, for ourselves and for those around us. But when we practice nonattachment, we discover a kind of freedom we didn't know was possible.

This is where contemplation can help. When we reflect on our desires, our attachments, and the emotions they stir, we begin to see them for what they are: temporary, ever-changing, and often less essential than they seem.

Understanding Nonattachment: Holding Life Lightly

Nonattachment isn't about giving up everything or detaching from joy. It's about creating a healthier relationship with our desires—one where we can enjoy things without being ruled by them.

Imagine floating down a river. If you try to grab on to every branch, rock, and vine along the way, you'll get stuck. But if you trust the flow and let yourself move with the current, the journey becomes easier. That's nonattachment—learning to flow rather than grasp.

When you release attachments, you make room for new experiences, allow yourself to grow, and free yourself from the suffering caused by unmet expectations. You begin to embrace the beauty of impermanence, knowing that life is constantly shifting.

Contemplative Practices: Seeing Desire for What It Is

One of the most powerful ways to develop nonattachment is through mindful reflection. When we take time to sit with our thoughts and observe our desires, we start to see them for what they really are—fleeting, impermanent, and often not as urgent as they seem.

Try this simple contemplation on impermanence:

1. Pick something you feel attached to—whether it's a goal, an object, or another person's approval.

2. Ask yourself what would happen if you didn't have it. Notice any emotions that arise.

3. Imagine life without it. Would your world fall apart, or would you adapt?

4. Recognize that everything changes. That thing you're holding on to now may not even matter in a year or five years.

5. Take a deep breath and let it be. You don't have to force yourself to detach—just noticing the temporary nature of things is enough to begin loosening their hold.

With regular practice, this kind of contemplation helps you realize that most of what you cling to isn't as permanent or necessary as it seems. That realization can be liberating.

Emotional Responses: The Power of Awareness

If you've ever felt frustration when something didn't go your way, you've experienced attachment in action. It's that tight, uncomfortable feeling when reality doesn't match expectations.

Nonattachment doesn't mean suppressing emotions. It means understanding them.

The next time you feel an emotional reaction to an unmet desire, try this:

1. Pause before reacting and take a deep breath.

2. Notice which emotion you're feeling—frustration, anxiety, fear.

3. Ask yourself what expectation is causing this reaction. For example, "I expected this person to understand me without me having to explain."

4. Reframe the thought. Instead of thinking, *This should not have happened,* try, *This is what happened. How can I respond with clarity instead of clinging to what I wanted?*

When you become aware of your emotional triggers, you can respond consciously instead of reacting automatically. This simple shift brings more emotional balance and helps you break free from the exhausting cycle of attachment and disappointment.

Exploring Inner Peace: The Freedom of Letting Go

Nonattachment leads to something many people seek: peace.

When we stop gripping so tightly—whether to our desires, our fears, or even our identity—we create space for something lighter. We begin to trust life rather than trying to control every detail.

Here are a few simple ways to practice letting go in daily life:

- **The one-minute release:** If you find yourself obsessing over something, set a timer for one minute. Breathe deeply, and with every exhale, imagine yourself letting go of the need to control or fix it.

- **The "Will this matter?" check-in:** When you catch yourself getting worked up over something, ask yourself, "Will this still matter in a month? A year?" If the answer is no, let it be.

- **Gratitude over grasping:** Instead of focusing on what's missing, take a moment to appreciate what's already here. Gratitude is one of the quickest ways to shift from attachment to contentment.

- **Surrender to the moment:** Whether you're stuck in traffic, dealing with a difficult person, or waiting for something to happen, try saying to yourself, "This is what's happening right now. I don't have to fight it." Accepting the present moment, just as it is, dissolves attachment to how you think things should be.

Living With Nonattachment: Embracing the Journey

Nonattachment isn't about having no desires. It's about having the freedom to experience life fully without being trapped by what we want.

It's knowing that we can love without clinging, hope without demanding, and strive without suffering. It's learning to appreciate things without needing them to stay the same.

Most importantly, peace doesn't come from getting everything we want—it comes from learning to be okay even when we don't.

When we practice contemplation, understand our emotional triggers, and shift our perspective, we begin to loosen our grip and move through life with greater ease. The journey becomes lighter, and we discover that real freedom is found not in controlling everything but in letting go.

Final Thoughts

Letting go is about setting yourself free.

If you've ever felt exhausted by the constant chase—always wanting, always waiting for something to feel complete—know that there's another way. Nonattachment doesn't mean we stop caring or lose our passion for life. It simply means we stop looking outside of ourselves for happiness.

When we release our tight hold on outcomes, we gain something far more valuable: the ability to be fully present, to appreciate what's already here, and to welcome life as it comes.

In the next chapter, we'll explore what happens when we truly let go—not just in small moments but in a way that transforms how we move through the world. We'll step beyond the cycle of craving and into something even better: lasting peace.

Chapter 3:
The Freedom of Letting Go (Nirodha)

Imagine you're carrying a heavy backpack full of old books, unfinished projects, painful memories, and the weight of every expectation you've ever placed on yourself or others have placed on you. You keep adjusting the straps, trying to shift the load, but no matter what, it's exhausting. You think, *I just have to keep carrying this.*

Now imagine someone gently asking, "What if you put it down?"

This is the essence of *nirodha*—the freedom that comes when we stop clinging. In Buddhism, *nirodha* is the third of the Four Noble Truths, and it teaches that suffering isn't just something we have to endure—it's something we can release (*The Four Noble Truths*, 2022). The concept isn't about becoming detached from life but rather learning to let go of the things that cause us unnecessary suffering: the expectations, the need for control, the stories we tell ourselves about how things should be.

Letting go doesn't mean we stop caring. It doesn't mean we stop loving, dreaming, or hoping. Instead, it's about loosening our grip—on resentment, on fear, on the idea that we need to hold on so tightly to be okay. Because peace isn't found in what we cling to; it's found in what we can release.

In this chapter, we'll explore what letting go really means in a Buddhist sense and why it's one of the most liberating practices you can cultivate. We'll also explore practical ways to begin releasing attachment in your daily life—because while the idea of letting go sounds good in theory, it's the practice of it that actually changes us.

There's no perfect way to let go. You only have to be willing to notice where you're holding on too tightly and start loosening your grip, one breath at a time.

Because the truth is, you're already free. You just have to let go enough to feel it.

Meditation Practices for Nonattachment

Letting go sounds great in theory, but in practice? It's hard. Our minds cling to thoughts, emotions, and memories like burrs on a hiking sock. Even when we want to release something, it can feel like our brains just won't cooperate.

That's where meditation comes in.

Meditation isn't about emptying your mind or floating off into a mystical void. The goal is to create space, to become aware of your attachments without letting them define you. And when you practice nonattachment in meditation, you start to carry that skill into your daily life. The more you loosen your grip in stillness, the more you can loosen your grip in conversations, relationships, and stressful moments.

Here are four simple but powerful meditation practices to help you build nonattachment.

Mindful Breathing: Anchoring in the Present

Think of your breath as a steady anchor in the ever-moving sea of life. When emotions surge, when thoughts spiral, when anxiety grips, the breath is always there, offering a place to return to. Mindful breathing brings clarity and calms the nervous system, teaching you to let go of the mental clutter that keeps you stuck.

1. Find a comfortable seated position. Close your eyes if that feels good.

2. Take a deep breath in through your nose, filling your belly. Exhale slowly through your mouth.

3. Now, shift your awareness to the way your body receives the breath. Feel how your chest gently expands. Notice the subtle

rise and fall of your belly. Let your breath guide you into the present.

4. If your mind wanders (which it will—that's what minds do), gently bring your focus back to your breath, like returning home after a long trip.

5. Continue for a few minutes, simply observing. No force, no effort—just breathing.

With time, this practice teaches you that you don't have to hold on to every thought or feeling. You can simply observe, exhale, and let it pass.

Loving-Kindness Meditation: Shifting From Attachment to Compassion

Attachment often comes from wanting to control—our relationships, our circumstances, even how people see us. But when we practice compassion, we replace the grip of control with the openness of connection. Loving-kindness meditation (*metta*) helps shift our focus from grasping to giving, from fear to love.

1. Sit comfortably, close your eyes, and take a few deep breaths.

2. Begin by silently saying to yourself: "May I be happy. May I be peaceful. May I be free from suffering."

3. Now, picture someone you love—a friend, a partner, a pet. Imagine sending them the same wishes: "May you be happy. May you be peaceful. May you be free from suffering."

4. Extend the circle more widely: Picture someone neutral, such as a stranger you passed today. "May you be happy. May you be peaceful. May you be free from suffering."

5. Finally, extend these wishes to someone you find difficult to love, reminding yourself that all beings experience struggles: "May you be happy. May you be peaceful. May you be free from suffering."

6. Rest in the warmth of this practice for a few more breaths.

This meditation teaches us that love isn't about possession—it's about freedom. The more we practice, the less we need things or people to be a certain way in order to feel peace.

Body Scan Meditation: Letting Go of Tension and Resistance

Sometimes, our attachments show up as physical tension—clenched jaw, tight shoulders, a stomach that never seems to relax. A body scan meditation helps us let go of resistance, not just in our minds but in our bodies as well.

1. Lie down or sit comfortably. Close your eyes and take a deep breath.

2. Bring your attention to your feet. Notice any sensations—warmth, tingling, tension. There's no need to change anything—just observe.

3. Slowly move your awareness up through your body: your calves, thighs, hips. Feel into any tightness, any gripping. With each breath, imagine softening.

4. Continue scanning upward—your stomach, chest, arms, and hands. Observe without judgment.

5. Finally, bring awareness to your jaw, your eyes, your forehead. If you sense tension, imagine it dissolving with each exhale.

6. Rest in this state of ease, allowing yourself to simply be.

The body holds onto stress, old emotions, and even past experiences. This practice teaches us that just as we can release tension from our muscles, we can release emotional attachments that no longer serve us.

Visualization: Releasing What Weighs You Down

The mind responds powerfully to imagery. Visualization can help us *see* ourselves letting go, making it easier to actually do so.

1. Close your eyes and imagine standing beside a gently flowing river. In your hands, you hold a small stone—this represents something you're struggling to let go of.

2. Feel the weight of it. Notice what emotions arise as you hold on to it.

3. Now, imagine placing the stone in the water. Watch as the current carries it away—slowly, effortlessly.

4. Take a deep breath and notice how light your hands feel now, how free your body feels without the weight.

5. Open your eyes, carrying this sense of release with you into your day.

Sometimes, we need a tangible way to let go. This practice helps us visualize what release looks like, making it easier to embody in real life.

Final Thought: The Art of Loosening Your Grip

Letting go isn't a one-time event—it's a practice. Some days, it will feel effortless, like exhaling. Other days, you'll catch yourself gripping tightly, and that's okay. The key is to return. To breathe. To soften.

Meditation won't make you instantly detached from every worry or expectation. But it *will* give you a space to notice when you're holding on too tightly—and the choice to let go.

And that? That's real freedom.

Experiencing Peace Through Letting Go

We spend so much of our lives grasping—clinging to relationships, memories, expectations, and the illusion of control. We hold on to things because we believe they give us stability, certainty, and meaning. But in reality, it's the holding on that creates tension, anxiety, and suffering. True peace isn't found in controlling life—it's found in allowing it to unfold.

Letting go centers on giving yourself permission to be free. To loosen your grip on what you can't change. To trust the flow of life rather than fight against it. And when you begin to practice this, even in small ways, you'll discover something profound: Peace isn't something you chase—it's something you uncover by releasing what weighs you down.

Understanding Impermanence: The Beauty of the Temporary

Everything changes. The seasons shift, our bodies age, friendships evolve, and emotions rise and fall. The coffee you enjoy today will be gone tomorrow. The worry that kept you up last night will fade in a week.

This is impermanence, and while it might sound unsettling, it's actually liberating. When we understand that nothing lasts forever, we stop clinging so desperately. We soften. We appreciate.

Think of a sunset. You don't try to hold on to it—you simply enjoy it while it lasts. Life is the same way. When you accept that everything is temporary, you experience more joy in the present moment rather than fearing its loss.

Try this reflection: Think about something in your life that once felt so important, but that now barely crosses your mind. Maybe it was a heartbreak, a job you lost, or a phase of life you thought would last forever. Recognizing how things naturally shift can remind you that whatever you're holding on to today—whether it's a fear, an expectation, or an outcome—will also change in time.

Accepting Change: Flowing With Life Instead of Fighting It

Resisting change is like trying to stop a river with your hands. The more you push against it, the more exhausted you become. But when you step back and allow the water to flow, you realize it was never yours to control in the first place.

The truth is, change isn't the enemy—our resistance to it is. We suffer when we cling to what was or fear what will be. But when we embrace change as an inevitable part of life, we create space for peace, growth, and new possibilities.

- "What is one area of my life where I'm resisting change?"

- "What might happen if I softened my grip and allowed it to unfold naturally?"

Sometimes, what feels like an ending is actually a beginning. Holding on to the past can keep us from stepping into something even better.

Releasing Control: The Freedom in Surrender

Most of us like to think we have control over things—our relationships, our careers, the way life unfolds. But the truth? Control is often an illusion. The more we try to manipulate outcomes, the more we create stress, frustration, and disappointment.

Real peace comes when we learn to trust, to let go of the need to force things and allow life to unfold as it's meant to. This doesn't mean we stop caring or taking action—it means we stop gripping so tightly to how things "should" go.

- "I release the need to control. I trust the flow of life."

And then? Take a deep breath and allow yourself to *believe it.*

Transformative Reflection: Learning From Letting Go

Every time you've let go of something in the past, you've grown. Even the most painful losses have shaped you into who you are today. Letting go isn't about erasing the past—it's about using it as fuel for a wiser, more peaceful version of yourself.

Think about a time when you finally released something—a grudge, an expectation, an unhealthy attachment. How did it feel? Lighter? Freer? That feeling is the peace that comes from letting go.

Reflection Exercise

- In a journal, write about a time when you had to let go of something. What did it teach you?

- How did it change you?

- What can you take from that experience to help you let go now?

Final Thoughts

Peace doesn't come from having a perfect life. It comes from loosening your grip on the things that create suffering. It comes from trusting that even when things fall apart, you will be okay.

Letting go isn't something you do once—it's something you return to again and again. Some days, it will feel effortless. Other days, you'll catch yourself clinging, and that's okay. The key is to notice, breathe, and soften your grip.

Because when you stop resisting the flow of life, you don't just find peace—you *become* it.

Letting go isn't about becoming indifferent or detached from life—it's about fully embracing it without the weight of unnecessary suffering. It's realizing that peace isn't something you need to find—it's something you uncover when you stop clinging to the things that keep you stuck.

Through mindful breathing, we've learned to anchor ourselves in the present moment, finding clarity in each inhale and exhale. Through loving-kindness meditation, we've shifted from attachment to compassion, replacing grasping with genuine connection. With body awareness and visualization, we've practiced softening our grip—on tension, expectations, and the illusion of control. And in embracing impermanence, we've seen how acceptance of change opens the door to freedom.

Each time we release, even just a little, we step closer to peace.

But letting go is only one piece of the journey. To truly live with wisdom and clarity, we must also learn to see—to perceive life as it really is rather than how we wish it to be.

In the next chapter, we explore Right View—the ability to see ourselves, others, and the world without illusion. We'll uncover the filters that cloud our perception, the beliefs that shape our reality, and the transformative power of viewing life through the lens of wisdom and compassion. Because when we see clearly, we don't just let go—we awaken.

Chapter 4:

Seeing the World Clearly (Right View—Samma Ditthi)

Picture yourself looking through a foggy window. The world outside is there, but it's distorted, blurred, and unclear. Maybe you think you see something—an obstacle, a danger, a solution—only to realize that your perception was off when the fog begins to lift. This is how many of us move through life: reacting to situations based on assumptions, fears, and old habits rather than seeing things as they truly are.

Right View, the first step on the Buddhist Eightfold Path, is about learning to wipe that window clean. It's not about forcing ourselves to be positive or pretending life is always wonderful. It's about seeing reality—our joys, our struggles, and our suffering—with honesty and wisdom.

In this chapter, we'll break down the Four Noble Truths in a way that makes sense for modern life. We'll explore what it really means to suffer (and no, it's not just about big, dramatic pain), how our cravings and attachments keep us stuck, and what steps we can take to free ourselves from cycles of stress and dissatisfaction. Most importantly, we'll talk about how cultivating Right View doesn't mean striving for some perfect, enlightened state—it's about gently training our minds to see things more clearly, little by little, moment by moment.

Seeing the world clearly starts with simple shifts in perspective: questioning the stories we tell ourselves, pausing before reacting, and choosing curiosity over judgment. With time, these small shifts add up, lifting the fog and allowing us to meet life with greater peace, understanding, and ease. Let's begin.

Journaling Real-Life Examples of Suffering and Peace

If you've ever had a conversation with an old friend and suddenly realized how much you've changed, you've already experienced the power of reflection. It's easy to get caught up in the daily whirlwind of responsibilities, emotions, and reactions, but when we pause to look back—really look—we start to notice patterns. We see the ways in which we repeat cycles of suffering, and we also notice moments of peace, however fleeting.

Journaling is one of the simplest yet most powerful tools for gaining clarity on your experiences. It's not about writing perfect sentences or pouring out pages of deep, poetic wisdom. It's about capturing your own reality—your struggles, your moments of ease, and the space in between. When you take time to reflect on suffering and peace in your life, you begin to see the inner workings of your own mind. You become an observer rather than just a participant, and that shift alone can open the door to change.

Understanding Personal Experiences

Suffering isn't always dramatic. Sometimes, it's as subtle as the tension you feel when your phone pings with an email you don't want to answer. Other times, it's the dull ache of loneliness, regret, or feeling stuck in old habits. Journaling about these experiences can help you pinpoint what truly causes distress in your life. Is it external pressures? Self-imposed expectations? The fear of change? By recognizing these triggers, you can begin developing healthier ways to respond to them.

On the other side, peace is often overlooked because it tends to be quiet. The warmth of morning sunlight on your face, a deep breath after a long day, the feeling of connection in a shared moment with someone you love—these are moments of peace. Writing about them helps you recognize what fosters calm in your life so you can intentionally cultivate more of it.

Exploring Interconnectedness

When you journal, you don't just explore your own suffering—you also begin to see how it connects you to others. Every person you meet is carrying something unseen, struggling with worries and longings just like you. Reflecting on this shared human experience builds empathy, both for yourself and for those around you.

Try writing about a time when someone's kindness eased your suffering. Or a time when you felt comforted by the knowledge you weren't alone in your struggles. These reflections don't just deepen self-awareness; they remind you that suffering isn't an isolated experience. When you understand this, you become more compassionate toward both yourself and others.

Transforming Experiential Insights

Journaling can center around identifying suffering and what you learn from it. When you track your thoughts over time, you begin to notice shifts. Maybe a situation that once triggered anxiety no longer has the same power over you. Maybe you handled a recent conflict with more patience than you would have a year ago.

When we document our experiences, we start to see that suffering isn't just something to endure—it's something that can teach us. When we make the choice to reflect on how challenges shape us, we turn our struggles into sources of wisdom. This process builds a growth mindset, making us more resilient to future difficulties.

Creating an Ongoing Practice

Like any practice, journaling is most effective when done consistently. It doesn't have to be an elaborate ritual—just a few minutes a day can make a difference. Some people prefer to free-write, letting thoughts flow naturally. Others might use prompts, like the following:

- What was a moment of suffering I experienced today?

- What triggered it, and how did I respond?

- Did I experience peace today? What brought it about?

- What patterns am I starting to notice?

Over time, this habit becomes a reflective retreat—an opportunity to step back from the chaos of daily life and return to clarity. The more you engage in this practice, the more you train yourself to see your experiences clearly, making it easier to navigate life's inevitable ups and downs.

Right View isn't something we master overnight. It's a way of seeing that becomes clearer with practice. Through journaling, we gently train our minds to recognize suffering without being consumed by it, to appreciate peace without clinging to it, and to welcome life as it is—with wisdom, awareness, and an open heart.

Contemplation Exercises for Clear Perception

Clarity isn't something we stumble upon by accident. It's something we cultivate—like a lens we polish over time, revealing what was always there but often unseen. In Buddhism, one of the most powerful ways to develop this clarity is through contemplation. Unlike passive reflection, contemplation is an active practice: It invites us to turn ideas over in our minds, to sit with them, to let them unfold in ways that bring deeper understanding.

If you've ever reread a book or rewatched a movie and caught something you hadn't noticed before, you already understand the value of looking at something with fresh eyes. The same applies to Buddhist teachings and our everyday experiences. Contemplation helps us perceive reality more clearly—beyond assumptions, beyond habits, beyond surface-level reactions. The following exercises are designed to guide you in sharpening your perception, allowing you to see life with greater awareness and wisdom.

Practicing Mindful Observation

One of the simplest yet most powerful ways to boost clarity is through mindful observation. The goal here isn't to analyze or judge—just to notice.

Start by choosing a simple experience: watching a candle flicker, observing a tree swaying in the wind, or even noticing the way your thoughts arise and pass. What do you see? What do you feel? When you practice this type of focused attention, you begin to recognize the fluid nature of reality—how nothing is static, how emotions shift, how sensations come and go.

You can also experiment with visualization. Imagine moments of suffering, craving, and peace. How do they feel in your body? How does your mind react? By creating mental images, you turn these abstract concepts into something more tangible; over time, you may notice that your reactions to them shift. Instead of pushing suffering away or chasing peace, you start to observe them both with greater ease.

Silent Reflection Time

We live in a world full of noise—external noise from conversations, social media, and responsibilities, but also internal noise such as racing thoughts, worries, and expectations. Stepping into silence can feel unfamiliar at first, but it's within silence that clarity often emerges.

Set aside time for quiet reflection. This doesn't have to be a structured meditation session (though it can be). It can be as simple as sitting with a question: "What's causing me suffering right now?" or "How can I meet this moment with acceptance?"

In this stillness, insights arise—not because we force them, but because we allow space for them. Reflection nurtures patience, helping us accept life's constant changes instead of resisting them. Over time, this practice makes impermanence feel less like an idea and more like an embodied truth.

If you find silence challenging, consider contemplating in a group setting. Listening to others' reflections can offer fresh perspectives and remind you that the challenges of the mind are shared by many. A supportive space can provide both encouragement and accountability, making it easier to integrate these insights into your daily life.

Group Contemplation Practices

Contemplation doesn't always have to be a solitary practice. Engaging in group reflection can deepen our understanding by exposing us to different ways of thinking and experiencing the world.

In Buddhist traditions, many teachings are explored in community, where discussions serve as a means of deepening wisdom. When we share our insights, struggles, and questions, we not only clarify our own thoughts but also help others refine theirs.

Try joining (or creating) a small discussion group, even if it's informal. Choose a theme—such as suffering, impermanence, or mindfulness—and explore how these ideas show up in daily life. Sharing experiences and hearing others' reflections creates a sense of connection and reminds us that we're all learning together.

Through these contemplation exercises—whether practiced alone or in a group—you develop the ability to see things as they are rather than as you assume them to be. Clarity isn't about having all the answers; it's about learning to sit with questions, to observe without attachment, and to trust that, with time, understanding will unfold.

Final Thoughts

If there's one thing to take away from this chapter, it's this: Clarity isn't about having all the answers—it's about learning to see things as they truly are. Life is full of suffering, yes, but also peace. It's full of craving, but also contentment. The more we observe, reflect, and contemplate, the more we realize that we're not at the mercy of our struggles. We can understand them, work with them, and even learn from them.

Once we understand our suffering, the natural next question is: Now what? How do we respond? How do we live in a way that aligns with this newfound clarity?

That's where Right Intention comes in. If Right View is about seeing the world clearly, Right Intention is about choosing how to engage with it. It's about setting an intention to live with kindness, wisdom, and balance rather than being pulled around by old habits or unchecked desires.

In the next chapter, we'll explore how intention shapes our daily choices, our relationships, and even our happiness. You don't need to be perfect. You don't need to change everything overnight. But by committing—just a little—to ethical improvement and mindful living, you'll start to notice shifts. And those shifts? They have the power to change everything.

Let's take the next step together.

Chapter 5:
Finding Balance—Purpose, Heart, and Path
(Right Intention—Samma Sankappa)

What if I told you that everything you do—every choice, action, and even passing thought—carries the potential to shape your life? That every moment is an opportunity to realign with what truly matters to you? No pressure, right? Buddhism doesn't ask for perfection. It invites you to start where you are, with the life you have, and gently steer yourself in the direction of wisdom and compassion.

At the heart of this journey is Right Intention—the practice of moving through life with purpose, clarity, and a heart that aligns with what's good and meaningful. But the world is full of distractions, obligations, and situations that tug us in all directions. We're balancing careers, relationships, personal goals, and an overwhelming stream of daily decisions. How do we ensure that our intentions—not just our actions—are aligned with the person we truly want to be?

Right Intention isn't about lofty, unattainable ideals. It's about cultivating an inner compass that helps you make choices rooted in kindness, mindfulness, and integrity. It's not about forcing yourself to be "good" all the time but about bringing more awareness to why you do what you do. Imagine being able to pause before reacting, to step back before making a decision, and to approach life with more clarity and less regret. That's the power of Right Intention.

In this chapter, we'll explore how to build this mindset, why intention matters more than we think, and how small, daily shifts in our thinking can lead to profound changes in our well-being. By the end, you'll see that finding balance isn't about rigid discipline—it's about returning to yourself, again and again, with patience and purpose.

Setting Daily Intentions for Kindness

If you've ever had a stranger hold the door for you when your hands were full, received an unexpected compliment on a rough day, or had someone let you merge into traffic when they absolutely didn't have to, you know how a small act of kindness can change everything. These moments are tiny, almost imperceptible shifts in the grand scheme of life, but they hold weight. They make the world feel a little softer, a little safer.

Now, place yourself in the position of being the one who creates those moments—every day, in small but meaningful ways. That's the power of setting a daily intention for kindness.

Practicing kindness isn't just about being nice to others (though that's a great start). It's about actively choosing to engage with the world in a way that nurtures goodwill, strengthens relationships, and ultimately helps you feel more balanced and at peace. When kindness becomes a conscious intention rather than an afterthought, it changes from a passive trait into a guiding principle.

The Benefits of Daily Kindness

Daily kindness not only strengthens the lives of those around us but also enriches our own, creating a more compassionate world one small act at a time. Here are some specific examples:

- **Kindness creates positive ripples:** Every time you choose kindness, whether through a smile, a thoughtful message, or simply a moment of patience, it sets off a chain reaction. Your kindness may inspire someone else to pass it on, creating a ripple effect that reaches far beyond what you can see. And even if it doesn't? You've still added something good to the world—and that alone is enough.

- **Kindness strengthens relationships:** Whether with loved ones, coworkers, or even strangers, kindness builds trust and connection. It opens the door to deeper, more meaningful

42

interactions. People are drawn to warmth and sincerity, and when you make kindness a habit, you naturally build stronger relationships.

- **Kindness boosts mental and emotional well-being:** Neuroscience backs it up: Acts of kindness release oxytocin, a hormone that helps reduce stress and increase feelings of happiness. Studies have shown that people who engage in regular acts of kindness experience lower levels of anxiety and depression (Fryburg, 2021). It turns out that being kind doesn't just help others—it's also one of the simplest ways to improve your own emotional health.

- **Kindness builds resilience against stress:** Life can be overwhelming, but a mindset rooted in kindness can help you navigate it with more grace. When you intentionally choose kindness, even on difficult days, it shifts your focus away from stressors and toward what you can control—your response. Kindness creates inner calm, helping you handle challenges with more patience and less frustration.

How to Start Practicing Daily Intentions for Kindness

Here are some simple yet effective ways to cultivate daily intentions for kindness in your life:

- **Begin your day with a simple commitment:** Before you even get out of bed, set an intention: "Today, I will approach others with kindness. I will choose patience over frustration, understanding over judgment, and generosity over indifference."

- **Look for small opportunities:** Kindness doesn't have to be grand. A genuine compliment, checking in on a friend, holding space for someone who needs to vent—these small gestures carry enormous power.

- **Practice self-kindness, too:** It's hard to give kindness to others when you're running on empty. Treat yourself with the same compassion you extend to those around you.

When you make kindness an intentional, daily practice, you're not just improving your interactions with others—you're shaping your own mindset and well-being. And over time, this conscious commitment to kindness will become second nature, making balance and purpose something you *live* rather than something you seek.

Creating a Kindness Ritual

Kindness is often thought of as something spontaneous—something that happens in the moment rather than something we intentionally plan. But when kindness becomes a ritual, it transforms from an occasional act into a daily practice that reinforces our values and helps us feel more balanced.

Think of a kindness ritual like any other habit you build into your routine, whether it's your morning cup of tea, a few minutes of stretching, or winding down with a book at night. The more you integrate it into your day, the more natural it becomes. And the more natural it becomes, the more you start seeing kindness not as something extra but as a core part of how you move through the world.

Why Kindness Rituals Matter

Rituals help structure our intentions and ensure that we follow through with what we value most. Establishing a kindness ritual can have the following impact:

- **Act as a daily reminder:** With everything that's competing for our attention, it's easy to forget to slow down and prioritize kindness. A ritual keeps it front and center.

- **Strengthen our commitment to ethical living:** Kindness isn't just about being polite—it's about aligning our actions with the values we want to uphold.

- **Reinforce balance and stability:** Acts of kindness bring a sense of inner peace, counterbalancing the stress and distractions of daily life.

So, how do we actually build a kindness ritual into our lives?

How to Create Your Own Kindness Ritual

The best kindness rituals are simple, repeatable, and personal to you. Here are a few ideas to get started:

- **Begin each morning with a kindness intention:** Before you even get out of bed, set a small goal for the day. Ask yourself, "Who can I uplift today?" It could be something as simple as offering a sincere compliment or reaching out to a friend.

- **Tie kindness to an existing habit:** The easiest way to build a new ritual is to link it to something you already do. If you have a morning coffee routine, use that time to send a quick text of appreciation to someone in your life.

- **Start a kindness jar:** Each day, write down one act of kindness you did or witnessed and drop it into a jar. Over time, you'll have a tangible reminder of the positive impact you've made.

- **Commit to a weekly kindness challenge:** Choose one small act of kindness to focus on each week. Maybe it's letting someone go ahead of you in line, leaving a kind note for a coworker, or donating to a cause.

When kindness becomes part of your daily rhythm, it's no longer just an action—it becomes an expression of who you are.

Tracking Acts of Kindness: The Power of Reflection

Kindness is most powerful when it's intentional. And one way to make it even more intentional is to track it. Keeping a simple kindness journal—or even just taking a moment to reflect at the end of the day—can help bring more awareness to the impact of your actions and reinforce your commitment to living with purpose.

Why Tracking Kindness Works

Tracking your acts of kindness isn't about keeping score; it's about staying mindful and making kindness a consistent part of your life. When you write down the moments where kindness showed up—whether given or received—you start to notice just how much goodness exists around you. Here's why tracking helps:

- **It increases awareness and commitment:** Writing things down helps solidify them in your mind. The more you reflect on kindness, the more opportunities you'll start seeing to practice it.

- **It boosts motivation:** Seeing a growing list of acts of kindness—even small ones—can be a powerful motivator to keep going.

- **It deepens self-reflection:** Looking back on your kindness journal can reveal which types of kindness resonate most with you. Do you love offering words of encouragement? Helping strangers? Supporting friends? These insights can shape how you bring kindness into your life.

- **It holds you accountable:** Setting an intention is one thing—following through is another. A kindness journal creates a sense of responsibility for living out your values.

Simple Ways to Track Your Kindness

If journaling feels overwhelming, don't worry—tracking kindness doesn't have to be complicated. Here are a few easy ways to do it:

- **Write it down:** In a small notebook, jot down one act of kindness each day, whether it's something you did or something you received.

- **Make a kindness checklist:** Create a simple list of small kindnesses (e.g., "Smiled at a stranger," "Sent an encouraging text," "Let someone go ahead in line") and check them off as you go.

- **Reflect at the end of each month:** Look back at your acts of kindness and ask yourself, "How did these moments make me feel? How did they impact others? What did I learn?"

Tracking kindness helps turn good intentions into lasting habits. Over time, these small acts will create a ripple effect—not just in the lives of others, but in your own sense of balance and fulfillment.

Aligning Personal Values With Ethical Paths

Life feels a lot smoother when our actions align with what truly matters to us. When we live in harmony with our values, our decisions feel clearer, our relationships feel more authentic, and we move through the world with a sense of integrity. But modern life doesn't always make it easy. We're constantly bombarded with conflicting pressures: career demands, family expectations, social norms, and personal ambitions that don't always fit neatly together. It's easy to feel pulled in different directions, making choices that don't quite sit right with us.

That's where Right Intention steps in. Buddhism teaches that living ethically isn't about memorizing a rulebook or striving for perfection. It's about consistently checking in with ourselves, aligning our actions with our core values, and making choices that reflect the kind of person we truly want to be.

Identifying Key Values: Your Inner Compass

Before we can align our actions with our values, we first need to know what those values actually are. Sometimes, we assume we know what we stand for—until we're faced with a tough decision and suddenly feel torn. That's why taking time to reflect on our values is crucial.

Here's why identifying your key values matters:

- Reflection is the first step toward ethical alignment. When you pause to consider what truly matters to you, you gain a clearer sense of direction.

- Core values help you navigate choices mindfully. Instead of reacting impulsively, you can make intentional decisions that align with your deepest beliefs.

- Personal values serve as a compass for ethical living. They act as a guide, helping you stay consistent in your actions even when life gets chaotic.

- Aligning choices with values reduces conflict and increases satisfaction. When your actions contradict your values, you feel uneasy—like you're out of sync with yourself. When they align, your feel more at peace.

So, how do you identify your key values? Start by asking yourself these questions:

- "What qualities do I admire in others?"

- "When do I feel most proud of myself?"

- "What decisions have I made that I regret, and why?"

- "What impact do I want to have on the world around me?"

Once you've clarified your values, the next step is ensuring your daily choices reflect them. That's where an ethical decision-making framework comes in.

Ethical Decision-Making: A Framework for Intentional Choices

It's one thing to know your values—it's another to consistently act on them, especially when faced with difficult choices. An ethical decision-making framework provides structure, helping you assess situations with clarity and confidence rather than getting swept up in emotions or external pressures.

Here's why an ethical framework is helpful:

- It offers a structured approach to decision-making. Instead of making decisions on the fly, we can slow down and consider our options carefully.

- It supports thoughtful, intentional choices. A framework encourages us to pause, reflect, and make decisions in alignment with our values.

- It helps us assess the impact of decisions on ourselves and others. Ethical living isn't just about personal gain—it's about considering how our actions affect the people and world around us.

- It enhances our clarity and confidence when navigating dilemmas. When we have a process for decision-making, we feel more grounded and less uncertain.

A Simple Ethical Decision-Making Framework

When faced with a decision, try using this three-step process:

1. **Pause and reflect:**

   o What are my core values?

   o Does this choice align with those values?

   o What emotions are influencing my decision right now?

2. **Consider the consequences:**

   o How will this decision impact me in the short and long term?

   o How will it affect others?

   o Will I feel at peace with this choice later?

3. **Choose with integrity:**

   o Is this decision consistent with the person I want to be?

   o Am I making this choice out of fear, guilt, or obligation—or from a place of wisdom and kindness?

   o If I were explaining this decision to someone I respect, would I feel proud of it?

Aligning personal values with ethical action isn't always easy, but it's always worth it. The more we practice, the more natural it becomes—until one day, we realize that living with intention is no longer something we have to think about. It's simply who we are.

Practicing Integrity: Living Your Values Every Day

It's one thing to know your values—it's another to actually live by them. Integrity is the bridge between what we believe and how we act. It's not just about doing the right thing when people are watching; it's about staying true to ourselves even when no one else will ever know the difference.

In a world that constantly pressures us to compromise, practicing integrity is a radical act. It means making choices that align with our beliefs, even when it's inconvenient or uncomfortable. It means showing up as the same person in every area of life—at home, at work, in friendships, and in moments when no one's looking.

Why Integrity Matters

Integrity isn't just about being honest—it's about creating a life that feels whole and aligned. When we act in accordance with our values, we create the following:

- **A stronger sense of self-trust:** Every time we honor our values, we reinforce trust in ourselves. We become more confident in our choices and less dependent on external validation.

- **Deeper, more trusting relationships:** Whether in personal friendships or professional settings, people naturally trust those who act with integrity. Demonstrating consistency in our values builds reliability and strengthens bonds.

- **A greater sense of purpose and contentment:** When our actions match our beliefs, life feels more meaningful. There's less inner conflict, less second-guessing, and a greater sense of fulfillment.

- **Balance amid life's challenges:** When life throws curveballs, integrity serves as an anchor. It helps us make decisions with clarity and navigate difficulties with a steady heart.

Practicing integrity isn't about perfection—it's about awareness. We won't always get it right, but the key is noticing when we stray from our values and gently bringing ourselves back.

Adapting Values Over Time: The Power of Growth

While integrity is about staying true to our values, it's important to recognize that our values themselves can evolve. The person you were five years ago likely had different priorities, perspectives, and beliefs from the person you are today. Growth is a natural part of life, and so is the refinement of our values.

Some values remain constant—things like honesty, kindness, and respect. But others shift as we gain new experiences, meet new people, and see the world in new ways. The key is to stay open to this evolution rather than clinging rigidly to past beliefs.

Why Embracing Change in Values Is Important

Embracing change in our values is crucial for personal growth. Regular self-reflection helps us live intentionally instead of simply going through the motions based on outdated beliefs. By allowing our values to evolve, we remain open to new experiences, perspectives, and opportunities for learning.

As we grow and adapt, our decision-making becomes more nuanced and thoughtful, leading to more informed and ethical choices. Additionally, taking the time to examine our values deepens our self-awareness, giving us a clearer understanding of who we are and what truly matters in our lives.

How to Reflect on Your Evolving Values

To reflect on your evolving values, start by asking yourself which values feel most important to you right now and if any have shifted over the past year. It's also important to pay attention to any discomfort you might feel—if a decision seems out of sync, it could indicate that your values are changing.

Stay curious by being open to learning from different perspectives, challenging old beliefs, and exploring new ideas. Finally, revisit your ethical framework; as your values evolve, you may need to adjust your decision-making process accordingly.

Growth doesn't mean abandoning your integrity—it means refining it. When you give yourself permission to evolve, you move through life with greater wisdom, more flexibility, and a deeper sense of authenticity.

Final Thoughts

Living with Right Intention centers around getting intentional. It's about waking up each day and deciding, "How do I want to move through the world?" It's about checking in with yourself, aligning your choices with your values, and creating a life that feels balanced and true.

But intention isn't just about what we think—it's about what we say. Words shape relationships, define our character, and set the tone for how we connect with the world. That's why the next step on this journey is Right Speech—the practice of speaking truthfully, kindly, and with purpose.

In the next chapter, we'll explore how the words we choose can either build bridges or create distance, how mindful communication fosters stronger relationships, and how we can all practice speaking with more clarity, kindness, and integrity. After all, intention without action is just a wish. Let's take the next step—one word at a time.

Chapter 6:
The Power of Words
(Right Speech—Samma Vaca)

Words shape our world. They can build bridges or burn them down, heal wounds or create them, lift someone up or leave them feeling small. And yet, how often do we pause before speaking? How often do we ask ourselves: "Is what I'm about to say true? Is it kind? Is it necessary?"

In Buddhism, the concept of Right Speech—one of the eight steps on the Noble Eightfold Path—doesn't center around being overly polite or censoring ourselves into silence. It's about being mindful of the words we choose because they have power (*The Noble Eightfold Path*, n.d.). A careless comment can linger in someone's heart for years, while a few sincere words of encouragement can change the course of a person's life.

This chapter is an invitation to become more intentional with your speech—not just in what you say but in how you say it. We'll explore practical ways to cultivate honesty without cruelty, kindness without pretense, and wisdom without arrogance. The goal isn't to be perfect—because no one is—but to begin noticing how your words affect both yourself and others.

By the end of this chapter, you'll have simple, achievable practices to help you communicate more truthfully, compassionately, and effectively. And as you start integrating those practices into your daily life, you may notice a shift—not only in your relationships but also in how you feel about yourself. When you align your words with wisdom and kindness, you create more harmony both inside and out.

So, let's begin—because the way we speak matters, more than we think.

Reflecting on Daily Speech Influences

Every word we speak leaves a mark—on others, on ourselves, and on the energy we carry into the world. Our daily speech isn't just background noise; it shapes our relationships, our inner peace, and even our sense of self. When we become more aware of the impact of our words, we begin to see that speaking isn't just about expression—it's about connection.

The Ripple Effect of Words

Think about a time when someone said something that truly lifted you up—maybe a simple "I believe in you" or "I see how hard you're trying." Those words likely stayed with you, offering warmth and encouragement long after they were spoken. Now, think about a time when words stung—a careless remark, an impatient comment, or a moment of harsh criticism. That, too, may have lingered, settling in your mind as doubt or hurt.

Our words don't vanish the moment we say them. They ripple outward, influencing emotions, relationships, and even how others see themselves. A single kind sentence can build trust, while a thoughtless one can create walls between us and those we care about. When we begin to recognize this power, we naturally start to pause before we speak, asking ourselves: "Is this helpful? Is this necessary?"—not as a way to control ourselves, but as a way to build relationships that are rooted in honesty and compassion.

Practicing Active Listening

Right Speech isn't just about the words we say—it's also about the words we receive. In many conversations, we're already forming our response before the other person has even finished talking. But real connection happens when we listen fully—not just to the words, but to the emotions beneath them.

Active listening means giving our full attention, setting aside assumptions, and being present with the person in front of us. It means pausing before we respond so we reply with care instead of reacting out of habit. When we listen deeply, we make space for empathy, for understanding, for conversations that don't just fill the silence but truly bring people closer.

With practice, mindful speech and listening become a daily habit—not something we have to force, but something that naturally arises from our growing awareness. Over time, we begin to notice a shift: our conversations feel lighter, our relationships become stronger, and our words carry more meaning. And the more we practice, the more we realize that the way we speak is one of the most powerful choices we make, every single day.

Practicing Active Listening and Mindful Communication

Right Speech isn't just about choosing the right words—it's also about making space for the words of others. How often do we find ourselves half-listening, thinking about our response while the other person is still speaking? In a world full of distractions and rapid-fire communication, truly listening is a skill—and a rare one at that.

Practicing Active Listening

Listening is just as powerful as speaking—sometimes even more so. When we listen fully, we're not just waiting for our turn to talk; we're showing someone that their words matter, that they're seen and heard. This kind of attention creates a foundation of trust, deepening relationships and fostering understanding.

Active listening means

- giving someone our full presence—no half-scrolling, no mentally drafting responses.

- letting go of assumptions and staying open to what's being said.

- pausing before responding, so we answer thoughtfully rather than react instinctively.

When we listen this way, something shifts. Conversations stop feeling like transactions and start feeling like connections. Misunderstandings become less frequent. And the people in our lives feel safer opening up because they know we're truly there with them, not just waiting for our turn to speak.

Mindful Communication

Just as we practice mindfulness when we meditate or focus on our breath, we can also bring mindfulness into the way we communicate. Being aware of our emotions before we speak can make all the difference in how we express ourselves—and how our words are received.

Think about a time you spoke from frustration or stress. Maybe the words that came out were sharper than intended. Maybe they caused harm, even though that wasn't your goal. Now, think about a time you paused, took a breath, and responded with intention. The outcome was probably very different.

Mindful communication helps us

- express ourselves with clarity and compassion.

- reduce the likelihood of causing unintentional harm with careless words.

- navigate tough conversations with more ease and understanding.

It's not about filtering ourselves into perfection—it's about slowing down just enough to notice, "What am I feeling right now? How do I want to communicate this?"

When we combine active listening with mindful speech, something profound happens. Our conversations become richer. Our relationships grow stronger. And we start to experience communication as a source of connection rather than conflict. Over time, this awareness becomes second nature, helping us create a world—one conversation at a time—that's kinder, clearer, and more compassionate.

Reflecting on Past Conversations

Every conversation leaves behind an imprint. Some linger as warm memories—kind words exchanged, moments of genuine connection. Others replay in our minds with a tinge of regret—the thing we shouldn't have said, the words we wish we'd chosen differently, the silence we wish we'd filled.

Reflecting on past conversations shouldn't focus around dwelling on mistakes or overanalyzing every word. Instead, focus on recognizing patterns. When we pause to look back at how we communicate—both the good and the not-so-good—we gain valuable insight into ourselves.

What Can We Learn From Our Words?

Every interaction teaches us something. Maybe we realize we tend to interrupt when we're excited. Maybe we notice we soften our truth to avoid conflict. Or maybe we recognize that when we're tired or stressed, our patience shortens and our words lose their gentleness.

Looking back on past conversations helps us

- identify areas where we want to grow—whether that's speaking with more confidence, pausing before reacting, or practicing more honesty.

- understand the impact of our words—how they affect our relationships and how we feel after saying them.

- strengthen our ability to choose words that reflect who we want to be, not just how we feel in the moment.

Moving Forward With Awareness

Reflection is less about self-criticism and more about awareness. The more we observe our patterns, the more we can shift them. Instead of falling into the same communication habits, we can make conscious choices.

For instance, if we spoke out of frustration, we can learn to pause the next time. If we avoided saying what needed to be said, we can practice speaking up with kindness. If we were dismissive or distracted, we can remind ourselves that presence is a gift.

Right Speech doesn't expect perfection; it requires intention. With each conversation, we have the opportunity to grow—not just in how we communicate with others but in how we communicate with ourselves.

Replacing Harmful Words With Kindness

Let's say you've had a long day. Work was stressful, the traffic was a nightmare, and by the time you walk through the door, all you want is five minutes of peace. But as soon as you step inside, you see the sink overflowing with dishes, even though you specifically asked your partner to take care of it.

Before you even think, the words come out:

"Seriously? You couldn't wash a single dish? Do I have to do everything around here?" you bark.

The reaction? Defensiveness. Maybe your partner snaps back, maybe they shut down, but one thing's certain—no one feels good. The frustration that started with the dishes has now spread into the entire evening.

Now, let's rewind and take a breath. What if, instead of reacting, you paused? What if you softened your tone, adjusted your words, and approached the situation differently?

"Hey, I know we've both had a long day, but I'd really appreciate some help with the dishes. Can we take care of it together?"

Same situation, different approach—one that invites cooperation rather than conflict. And more often than not, when we offer kindness, it's mirrored back to us.

Now, let's take it inward. Imagine you're trying something new—maybe a skill, a hobby, or even just making a habit change. The first attempt doesn't go well. Maybe you forget, mess up, or fall short of your own expectations. Your first instinct? Self-criticism.

"Ugh, I'm so bad at this. Why do I even try?"

But what if you replaced that with kindness?

"I'm learning. It's okay to take time. I'll get better with practice."

It might feel small, but over time, these shifts add up. They change how we experience the world, how we treat others, and, most importantly, how we treat ourselves. Because when we make kindness a habit—in our words and in our thoughts—we don't just create more positive conversations. We create a more compassionate life.

Words are powerful—they can heal or harm, build or break. And the truth is, we don't always realize the weight of what we say until it's already out in the world. Sometimes, it's a sharp comment said in frustration. Other times, it's the way we speak to ourselves—critical, impatient, unkind. It's important to understand that just as words can cause harm, they can also create profound change. By becoming aware of how we speak, we can shift from negativity to kindness, fostering more positive and meaningful interactions.

Identifying Negative Language

The first step in changing our words is noticing them. We all have patterns in how we speak—whether it's criticism disguised as honesty, sarcasm that stings more than it amuses, or self-talk that tears us down instead of lifting us up. Recognizing these habits isn't about judgment; it's about awareness.

Ask yourself:

- "Do I tend to use negative or critical language when I'm stressed?"

- "Do my words encourage or discourage the people around me?"

- "How do I speak to myself—is it with kindness or harshness?"

Acknowledging these tendencies isn't a failure—it's an opportunity. The moment you become aware of your words, you gain the ability to change them.

Practicing Kindness in Speech

Once we notice negativity in our speech, we can begin to replace it with kindness. This doesn't mean avoiding difficult conversations or pretending everything is fine. It means speaking in a way that creates connection rather than conflict:

- Instead of criticism, we can offer encouragement:

  o Rather than: "You always forget to clean up."

  o Try: "I really appreciate it when you help keep things tidy."

- Instead of shutting someone down, we can offer understanding:

○ Rather than: "That's not a big deal, just get over it."

○ Try: "I see that this is really bothering you. Do you want to talk about it?"

Kind words don't just make others feel good—they shift the energy of an entire interaction. They create a space where people feel safe, valued, and understood.

Transformative Language Techniques

Kindness in speech isn't about sugarcoating the truth—it's about *how* we communicate it. A few simple shifts in language can completely change the tone of a conversation:

- **Use "I" statements instead of accusations:**

    ○ Instead of: "You never listen to me."

    ○ Try: "I feel unheard when I try to share something important."

- **Reframe complaints into constructive feedback:**

    ○ Instead of: "This is a disaster."

    ○ Try: "Let's find a way to make this work better."

- **Practice neutral, solution-focused language:**

    ○ Instead of: "You're wrong."

    ○ Try: "That's an interesting perspective—here's how I see it."

These small shifts encourage deeper conversations, reduce defensiveness, and cultivate emotional intelligence both in ourselves and in those we interact with.

Implementing Kindness in Daily Conversations

Kindness isn't just something we sprinkle into special moments—it's a daily practice. The more we choose words that uplift rather than tear down, the more natural it becomes. And the best part? Kindness is contagious.

Compliment freely; genuine praise has a lasting impact. Express gratitude by thanking someone for their effort, even in small things. Offer words of encouragement—sometimes, a simple "You've got this" can mean everything.

As we practice kindness in our speech, we begin to notice how others respond to us and how we feel. Conversations become lighter, relationships grow stronger, and we create a ripple effect that spreads beyond us. Kindness, once spoken, has a way of traveling far beyond what we can see.

Final Thoughts

If this chapter has shown us anything, it's that our words hold incredible power. They can strengthen relationships or strain them, uplift or discourage, bring clarity or confusion. The way we speak—to others and to ourselves—matters more than we often realize.

When we become mindful of our speech, practice active listening, and replace negativity with kindness, we create conversations that build connection rather than division. We begin to speak with intention rather than impulse, choosing words that reflect our values rather than just our emotions in the moment. And perhaps most importantly, we recognize that communication isn't about getting it perfect—it's about getting it better. A single mindful pause before we speak, a moment of listening before reacting, a shift from criticism to encouragement—

these small efforts add up, transforming not just our conversations but the relationships and communities we build around us.

However, Right Speech is just one part of the bigger picture. What we say is important, but so is what we do. Our actions—big and small—shape our path just as much as our words do. In the next chapter, we'll explore Right Action—what it means to live in alignment with our values, make choices that reflect who we truly are, and create a life that feels both meaningful and authentic. Because when our words and actions are in harmony, we don't just speak our truth—we live it.

Chapter 7:
Living True to Yourself
(Right Action—Samma Kammanta)

There's a moment in life—maybe many moments—when you wonder, *Am I really being true to myself?* It sneaks in when you say yes when you mean no, when you stay quiet when your heart tells you to speak, or when you make choices that don't sit well in your gut. Living with integrity—acting in alignment with your values—feels like a lofty goal, but in Buddhism, it's quite simple: Right Action.

Right Action is about the way we move through the world—not in a rigid rule-following sense, but in a way that creates inner peace and prevents unnecessary harm. It's less about perfection and more about intention. It centers around making choices that reflect the kind of person you want to be, even when no one's watching.

This chapter isn't here to tell you how to be good or hand you a list of dos and don'ts. Instead, we're going to explore how practicing Right Action can help you feel more at ease with yourself—less second-guessing, fewer regrets, and a deeper trust in the choices you make. It's about moving through life in a way that feels aligned, not forced.

You'll learn how small shifts in your daily actions can create a more peaceful mind and a lighter heart. We'll talk about what it means to act ethically in a modern world full of gray areas, how to handle mistakes without self-judgment, and how avoiding harm—toward yourself and others—can lead to an unshakable sense of self-respect.

Exploring Ethical Action Through the Five Precepts

Ethical action, an important aspect of Right Action, focuses on making choices that align with your values so you can move through life with a clear conscience and a steady heart. In Buddhism, this idea is blended into the Five Precepts, a simple yet powerful ethical framework that helps guide mindful choices in daily life (*The 5 Precepts*, 2019).

Think of the Five Precepts as a compass rather than a commandment list. They're not about judgment or perfection but about creating a life that feels lighter, more peaceful, and deeply aligned with who you want to be. Each precept serves as a reminder to act with care, toward both yourself and others. And the best part? You don't have to get it all right at once. The practice is in the effort, the awareness, and the small, intentional choices you make every day.

Let's break them down (*The 5 Precepts*, 2019):

1. **Do no harm (ahimsa):** This isn't just about avoiding physical harm—it includes your words, your actions, and even the way you treat yourself. When you move through life with kindness and consideration, you naturally experience less inner conflict and regret.

2. **Be honest:** Not just in what you say, but in how you live. Being truthful cultivates trust—with yourself and with others—so you don't have to carry the mental weight of dishonesty or misalignment.

3. **Respect your body and mind:** This precept invites you to be mindful of what you consume, whether it's food, substances, or even the media you engage with. It's about making choices that support your well-being instead of clouding your judgment.

4. **Honor relationships:** Whether it's with a partner, a friend, or a stranger, acting with integrity in your relationships promotes

connection and respect. It's about being conscious of your impact on others and choosing kindness over impulse.

5. **Practice generosity:** In this context, generosity isn't just about material giving—it's about offering your time, attention, and compassion. When you approach life with a spirit of generosity, you naturally create more meaningful connections and experience deeper fulfillment.

When you practice these precepts, even in small ways, you start to notice a change. Your mind feels clearer. Your relationships become healthier. And, most importantly, you begin to trust yourself more.

Living ethically aligns you to move through life in a way that feels honest, intentional, and free. And that kind of integrity? It's one of the greatest gifts you can give yourself.

Practical Application of the Precepts

The beauty of the Five Precepts is that they aren't meant to be abstract ideas floating somewhere in the realm of "things I should probably do but don't have time for." They're meant to be lived. And the best way to live them? One small conscious choice at a time.

Integrating the precepts into daily life doesn't require a life overhaul. You don't need to run away to a meditation yurt for hours to practice ethical living (although that doesn't sound terrible). It's about making conscious decisions that align with your values—decisions that, over time, create a sense of inner peace and personal integrity.

Here are a few simple ways to make the precepts a natural part of your life:

- **Make conscious choices in daily life:** Every action, no matter how small, is an opportunity to practice integrity. Before speaking, ask: "Is this true? Is it necessary? Is it kind?" Before making a decision, pause and ask yourself: "Will this bring harm to myself or others? Will it add to my peace or take away from it?" These small moments of awareness help align your actions with the person you truly want to be.

- **Reflect on your actions regularly:** Self-reflection isn't about self-criticism—it's about self-awareness. Taking a few minutes each day to check in with yourself can help you live more intentionally. Ask yourself: "Did my actions today reflect my values?" If not, that's okay. Awareness is the first step to change. Reflecting regularly helps reduce stress and guilt, because instead of being on autopilot, you're making choices that feel right in your heart.

- **Engage in meaningful conversations:** Talking about the precepts with others makes them more real. Whether it's with a friend, a partner, or a supportive community, discussing ethical dilemmas and mindful living reinforces their importance. It's not about preaching—it's about learning from each other, sharing experiences, and growing together. Plus, when you surround yourself with people who value integrity, it becomes easier to stay on track.

- **Approach growth with patience:** There will be moments when you act impulsively, say the wrong thing, or fall short of your intentions. That's normal because you're human. When you approach ethical living with curiosity instead of pressure, it becomes something you want to practice rather than something you feel you have to do.

The more you integrate these small practices, the more natural they become. And before you know it, living with integrity won't feel like effort—it will simply feel like you.

The Ripple Effect of Ethical Action

Every action we take, every word we speak, and every decision we make creates a ripple. Sometimes, those ripples are small and barely noticeable, like choosing patience instead of snapping at a barista who got your order wrong. Other times, they're big and life-changing, like standing up for what's right when it would be easier to stay silent.

When we act with integrity, those ripples don't just stay within us—they expand outward, shaping our relationships, communities, and even the way others choose to act. Ethical choices aren't just personal; they're contagious.

Ethical Behavior Inspires Others

When you choose kindness, honesty, and mindfulness in your actions, you set an example—whether you realize it or not. Have you ever noticed how a simple act of generosity, like someone paying for a stranger's coffee, can start a chain reaction? Or how seeing someone handle a difficult situation with grace makes you want to do the same?

Your ethical actions create a space where others feel encouraged to do the same. The way you treat people teaches them how to treat others. And that kind of impact? It's powerful.

Integrity Strengthens Connection

At its core, ethical living centers around building relationships based on trust, respect, and authenticity. When you consistently act in ways that align with your values, you develop a deeper sense of connectedness—not just with others but with yourself.

You no longer have to carry the stress of pretending to be someone you're not. You don't have to second-guess your decisions or wonder if you could have handled something better. Instead, you move through life with a sense of alignment, knowing that your actions reflect your true self.

Reflection Leads to Growth

One of the most rewarding aspects of practicing ethical action is looking back and seeing how far you've come. When you start to notice the positive effects of your choices—less stress, stronger relationships, a sense of ease within yourself—it becomes natural to continue.

And the more you reflect on the results of ethical action, the more you grow. You start to recognize patterns, understand what truly matters to you, and refine the way you show up in the world. It's a cycle of continuous improvement—one that leads to a life that feels honest, fulfilling, and full of purpose.

By living, you won't completely avoid harm, but you can focus on creating good. And the best part? The more you do it, the more good comes back to you.

Overcoming Challenges: Navigating the Realities of Ethical Living

I want to be clear that practicing ethical action isn't always easy. It sounds great in theory, but in real life? Temptation, frustration, and old habits don't just disappear overnight. Sometimes, doing the right thing feels inconvenient, uncomfortable, or even like it's working against you.

Maybe you catch yourself telling a little white lie to avoid an awkward conversation. Maybe you justify cutting corners because everyone else is doing it. Or maybe you know deep down that an action doesn't align with your values, but choosing differently feels really hard.

Truthfully, ethical living doesn't erase struggling. What it does is allow you to recognize when you're struggling and then make the choice to realign—over and over again. That's where growth happens.

Acknowledge the Temptations Without Shame

The first step in overcoming challenges is recognizing that they exist without beating yourself up for it. That's awareness.

Temptation to act outside of your values is normal. Maybe it's the urge to gossip because it makes you feel included. Maybe it's the temptation to bend the truth to make yourself look better. Instead of judging yourself, pause and ask: "Why am I feeling this pull?" That moment of reflection can be the difference between acting on impulse and choosing integrity.

Find Strength in Stories of Perseverance

We're all human, and we all struggle. That's why hearing stories of others who've handled ethical challenges can be so powerful.

Think about a time when someone stood by their values, even when it was hard—maybe a friend who refused to lie to get ahead, or someone who spoke up for what was right despite the risk. Those moments remind us that integrity isn't about the easy route; it's about the right one. And every time you make the harder, more ethical choice, you become that inspiration for someone else.

Create Accountability Systems

Sometimes, the best way to stay on track is to have people in your life who hold you to your values.

Accountability doesn't mean punishment—it means support. Maybe it's a friend you can check in with when you're struggling with a tough decision. Maybe it's journaling about your actions at the end of each day. Maybe it's simply setting a personal intention in the morning: "Today, I will act in a way that makes me proud."

When you create small systems that remind you of your commitment to ethical living, it becomes easier to stay the course.

There will be days when you mess up. That's part of being human. The key is not letting one mistake make you believe you've failed. Ethical living isn't all-or-nothing—it's a practice. Each moment gives you a new chance to choose integrity.

So, when you stumble, acknowledge it, learn from it, and try again. The goal isn't to never fall—it's to keep getting back up. And the more you do so, the stronger your commitment becomes.

Observing the Effects of Actions on Relationships

Our actions are like invisible messages we send to others. A kind gesture tells someone they matter. A broken promise tells them they can't rely on us. Speaking with honesty shows respect, while deception erodes trust. Even when we don't intend harm, the way we interact with others shapes how they feel and how they respond to us.

When we become aware of this, we naturally become more mindful in our interactions. We start asking ourselves questions like these:

- "How is my tone affecting the conversation?"

- "What message is my action sending?"

- "Am I contributing to trust or creating distance?"

Small, conscious choices—like being present in conversations, following through on commitments, or responding with patience instead of frustration—can change relationships from strained to strong.

Listening and Communication: The Heart of Ethical Interaction

We often think ethical action is about what we do, but just as important is how we communicate. Mindful communication is one of the most powerful ways to build trust and connection. Consider the following:

- **Active listening fosters understanding:** Instead of just waiting for our turn to talk, truly listening—without interrupting, judging, or planning a response—shows the other person that they matter.

- **Honest and respectful speech strengthens bonds:** Speaking with care, particularly when discussing difficult topics, creates an environment where people feel safe to open up.

- **Nonverbal cues matter:** A warm smile, a gentle nod, or even an open posture can say just as much as words. When our body language aligns with kindness, we naturally encourage positive interactions.

When we listen with presence, speak with honesty, and pay attention to the signals we send, relationships deepen. Ethical action, at its core, is about treating others in a way that nurtures—not depletes—our connections.

The More Mindful We Are, the Stronger Our Relationships Become

When we recognize how our actions and words impact others, we stop operating on autopilot. Instead of reacting impulsively, we respond with awareness. Instead of creating distance, we establish closeness. And the more we practice, the more natural it becomes.

Living ethically isn't just about making the "right" choices—it's about making choices that bring us closer to the people we care about. And in the end, isn't that what we all want?

Building Compassionate Relationships

At the heart of every strong relationship is one simple yet powerful force: compassion. When we approach our connections with kindness and consideration, something shifts. Walls come down, misunderstandings soften, and mutual respect grows. Ethical action isn't just about doing what's right—it's about nurturing relationships in a way that makes both people feel valued, seen, and understood.

Compassion isn't about always agreeing or avoiding difficult conversations. It's about recognizing that the person in front of you— whether it's a friend, a partner, a coworker, or a stranger—is just as human as you are. They have their own struggles, their own fears, their own moments of insecurity. When you choose to respond to others with understanding instead of judgment, you create a space where relationships can truly thrive.

Compassion Starts With Small Acts

Compassionate relationships aren't built on grand gestures— they're built on consistent, small moments of kindness:

- Listening without rushing to respond shows you care about the other person's thoughts.

- Choosing patience over frustration in difficult moments strengthens trust.

- Offering words of encouragement can be the difference between someone feeling alone and feeling supported.

When kindness becomes a habit, relationships become a source of warmth and ease instead of stress and conflict.

Navigating Conflicts With Ethics and Respect

No relationship is free from disagreements—but conflict doesn't have to be destructive. In fact, when handled with mindfulness, conflict can deepen relationships and build stronger bonds. The key? Approaching disagreements ethically and respectfully instead of reactively. Consider the following:

- **Pause before responding:** Before reacting in frustration, take a breath. Ask yourself, "Am I responding in a way that aligns with my values?" A moment of awareness can prevent a hurtful comment or unnecessary escalation.

- **Seek to understand, not just to be right:** Instead of focusing on proving a point, try to understand the other person's perspective. When both people feel heard, conflict turns into collaboration.

- **Use forgiveness as a tool for growth:** Holding on to resentment creates distance, but forgiveness—both of others and of ourselves—allows relationships to move forward. Forgiveness doesn't mean forgetting or excusing harm; it means choosing to release bitterness so healing can begin.

Reflecting on Our Actions to Cultivate Greater Compassion

Compassion grows when we take the time to reflect. Ask yourself:

- "Did my actions today contribute to kindness and understanding?"

- "Could I have handled a situation with more patience or empathy?"

- "How did my words impact the people around me?"

These small moments of reflection help us stay aware of our impact, making it easier to course-correct when needed. And the more we practice, the more compassion becomes second nature.

Compassion Strengthens Everything

Whether in friendships, romantic relationships, or everyday interactions, ethical action and compassion create deeper, more fulfilling connections. It's not about perfection—it's about consistently choosing kindness, even in challenging moments.

The way we treat others becomes the legacy we leave behind. And when that legacy is built on compassion? It has the power to transform not only our relationships but the world around us.

Final Thoughts

Practicing ethical action centers around making conscious choices that align with the person you want to be. Some days, it will feel effortless. You'll speak with kindness, act with integrity, and move through your relationships with compassion. Other days? You might slip up. You might react impulsively, say something you regret, or struggle with a decision that feels like it has no right answer. That's okay. This isn't about getting it right all the time. It's about awareness, intention, and growth.

In the next chapter, we'll explore Right Livelihood, the Buddhist principle of aligning your career with non-harming and ethical standards. Maybe you're choosing a profession, handling workplace challenges, or re-evaluating your career path. This practice invites you to ask yourself: "Does my work align with my values? Am I contributing to the well-being of others?"

While Right Action nurtures personal integrity, Right Livelihood extends that integrity into the wider world. Let's walk this path together.

Chapter 8:
Transforming Work Into a Source of Peace
(Right Livelihood—Samma Ajiva)

Most of us spend more time working than doing just about anything else—sometimes even sleeping. If you've ever counted down the minutes until the end of your shift, dreaded checking your emails, or fantasized about quitting your job and moving to a monastery (no judgment), then you already know that work can be a major source of stress. But what if work could be something more than just a paycheck? What if it could be a path to inner peace?

Buddhism offers us a guide to approaching our careers with mindfulness, ethics, and intention. This is where Right Livelihood—one of the principles of the Eightfold Path—comes in. Right Livelihood challenges us to reflect on whether the way we earn a living is in alignment with our values, contributes to the well-being of others, and does no harm. It's not about having the "perfect" job but about bringing awareness to what we do, how we do it, and why we do it.

But let's be real—most of us don't have the luxury of walking away from a job that pays the bills, even if it's not our dream job. The good news? Right Livelihood isn't about flipping your life upside down overnight. It's about small, intentional shifts that can transform your relationship with work, helping you feel more fulfilled, aligned, and at peace—even in an office that still insists on 8 a.m. meetings.

In this chapter, we'll explore how to bring Buddhist wisdom into your work life. Whether you're in a career you love, one that challenges you, or one that simply pays the rent, you'll learn how to cultivate meaning, integrity, and well-being in your professional life—without needing to change everything overnight. Because true transformation doesn't always come from quitting your job and moving to the mountains. Sometimes, it comes from learning how to approach each task, each challenge, and each workday with a little more presence, purpose, and peace.

Reflecting on Work Impacts and Ethics

Work isn't just something we do—it's something that shapes us. The tasks we complete, the people we interact with, and the systems we support all leave an imprint, not just on our own lives but on the world around us. Yet, in the hustle of deadlines, meetings, and the ever-growing inbox, it's easy to lose sight of why we do what we do and what impact it has.

Right Livelihood in Buddhism invites us to pause and reflect: "Is my work aligned with my values? Does it contribute to the well-being of others, or does it cause harm? Does it bring me a sense of purpose, or do I feel disconnected from its meaning?" These aren't always easy questions, but they are powerful ones.

Understanding Ethical Work

At its core, ethical work is about integrity—it's the practice of engaging in a profession that respects and uplifts rather than exploits or harms. But ethical work is more than just following laws or company policies. It's about fostering trust, respect, and purpose in how we show up each day. When our work aligns with ethical principles, we feel a deeper sense of fulfillment. We contribute to a healthier workplace culture, and we become part of something that feels meaningful rather than just routine.

Think about it—when you respect and trust the people you work with, doesn't everything flow a little more easily? Ethical workplaces create environments where collaboration, transparency, and mutual respect thrive. Whether you're in customer service, healthcare, tech, education, or any other field, the way you approach your work can have a ripple effect.

80

Consequences of Our Work

Every job has an impact, whether we realize it or not. A teacher shapes young minds, a doctor saves lives, a designer influences the way people interact with the world, and even a barista sets the tone for other people's morning. But the impact of work goes beyond the people we directly interact with—it also affects society, the environment, and future generations.

This doesn't mean we have to put pressure on ourselves to be perfect or single-handedly change the world. But it does mean acknowledging the role we play. What does your work contribute to? How does it affect your mental and emotional well-being? Does it align with the kind of world you want to help create? Taking the time to reflect on these questions can help us make more conscious, ethical career choices—whether that means making a small shift in how we approach our tasks or rethinking our long-term career goals.

Identifying Personal Values

When our work aligns with our values, we feel more authentic, motivated, and at peace. But to make that alignment happen, we first need to clarify what our values actually are. Ask yourself:

- "What matters most to me in a workplace (integrity, creativity, service, financial security)?"

- "Do I feel proud of what I do and how I do it?"

- "What kind of impact do I want my work to have on others?"

Values act as our internal compass, helping us navigate career decisions with greater clarity. They can also ground us when challenges arise—when work gets stressful, when we feel uncertain about our path, or when ethical dilemmas emerge. If we've already defined what's important to us, we can use those values to make choices that feel aligned rather than reactive.

Career Reflection Exercise: Aligning Work With Ethics

To bring this reflection into your practice, try this simple exercise:

- **Review your daily tasks:** Write down what you do in a typical workday. Then, next to each task, note how it impacts others—your coworkers, customers, the broader community. Are there any actions that feel out of alignment with your values? Any areas where you could bring more ethical awareness?

- **Identify your work's impact:** Consider the bigger picture. Does your work contribute to something you believe in? If you feel disconnected, how might you shift your role—through small choices or long-term goals—to create more alignment?

- **Engage in ethical conversations:** Start an ongoing dialogue about ethics in your workplace. It doesn't have to be a big debate—sometimes, just asking thoughtful questions can plant the seeds for change.

The goal isn't perfection but awareness—bringing more intention into how we work and the impact we have. Because when we do this, our careers become more than just jobs. They become opportunities to live our values, promote peace, and contribute to the world in a way that feels meaningful.

Exploring Alignment Between Career and Values

Have you ever had a job that just felt wrong—like you were constantly forcing yourself to care, but deep down, something wasn't clicking? Or maybe you've felt drained at the end of the day, not because the work was hard but because it didn't align with what truly matters to you? You're not alone. Many people go through their careers on autopilot, without pausing to ask themselves: "Is this work in line with my values?"

Buddhism teaches that Right Livelihood isn't just about avoiding harm—it's about actively creating work that reflects integrity and purpose. Finding that alignment between career and values isn't always easy, but when we do so, work transforms from something we endure into something that energizes us. This doesn't mean we all have to become monks or start nonprofits; every job has meaning when approached with the right mindset. The key is discovering how your career can be a reflection of what matters most to you.

Finding Your True Calling

Let's get one thing out of the way: Finding your "true calling" doesn't mean you have to know exactly what you want to do for the rest of your life. It's not a single, perfect job waiting for you like a hidden treasure. Instead, it's about recognizing what lights you up and what kind of work makes you feel engaged, purposeful, and alive.

Ask yourself:

- "What kinds of activities make me lose track of time?"

- "What issues or causes am I naturally drawn to?"

- "When do I feel most in alignment with myself?"

Aligning your work with your passions doesn't mean every day will be perfect, but it does mean you'll have an underlying sense of meaning and motivation. People who feel connected to their work tend to be more creative, resilient, and satisfied, even when challenges arise.

Creating a Values-Based Career Plan

Once you have a sense of your values and interests, the next step is building a career around them. This doesn't have to mean a drastic career change—it can be as simple as tweaking how you approach your current job or setting intentions for the future:

- **Clarify your values:** Write down your top five values. These might include honesty, creativity, service, sustainability, or balance.

- **Assess your current role:** Does your work align with these values? If not, are there ways to bring more of them into your daily tasks?

- **Set value-driven goals:** These don't have to be major shifts. Maybe it's finding a mentor in an ethical company, moving toward a leadership role where you can shape company culture, or even seeking work that better fits your passions over time.

- **Check in regularly:** Our careers evolve, and so do our values. Make a habit of reassessing your goals so you stay true to what matters.

When your work aligns with your values, it creates a deep sense of authenticity. You don't have to compartmentalize who you are at work and who you are in life—they become one and the same.

Practical Approaches to Ethical Choices

Even if you're not in a job that perfectly aligns with your values, there are small, intentional ways to bring more integrity into your work life:

- **Use a values checklist:** When making career decisions (choosing a new job, deciding on a project, handling a workplace dilemma), ask yourself: "Does this align with my core values?"

- **Lead by example:** You don't have to preach ethics to your coworkers, but when you quietly hold yourself to high standards—acting with kindness, honesty, and fairness—it creates a ripple effect.

- **Find your people:** Building connections with like-minded individuals at work or in your industry can provide support and motivation when you're trying to stay aligned.

Overcoming Obstacles to Alignment

Let's be real—aligning work with values isn't always smooth sailing. Sometimes, ethical concerns clash with workplace culture. Other times, financial realities make it difficult to shift careers. And let's not forget the internal doubts: *Am I being unrealistic? Will this even make a difference?*

Here's the key: Alignment doesn't mean perfection; it means persistence:

- **Recognize common barriers:** Workplaces are complex, and not every decision will be easy. But acknowledging potential conflicts ahead of time can help you navigate them more effectively.

- **Develop resilience:** When challenges arise, remind yourself why your values matter. Returning to your sense of purpose can help you stay grounded in difficult situations.

- **Embrace flexibility:** Sometimes, alignment doesn't happen all at once. Small steps—advocating for better practices at work, seeking a role that better matches your values, or shifting career direction over time—can add up.

At the end of the day, the goal isn't to find the perfect job. It's to build a career that resonates with who you are and what you stand for. That's what brings true fulfillment—not just in work, but in life.

Final Thoughts

If there's one thing to take away from this chapter, it's this: Your work is more than just a paycheck—it's a reflection of your values, your integrity, and your impact on the world. Whether you're in your dream job, just making ends meet, or somewhere in between, every day presents an opportunity to bring more awareness, ethics, and meaning into what you do.

Right Livelihood isn't about having a perfect career. It's about making conscious choices—big or small—that align with your values and allow you to work with integrity. Maybe that means shifting careers entirely. Maybe it means bringing more compassion into how you interact with your coworkers. Or maybe it's simply recognizing that your work has value, even if it doesn't always feel like it.

In the next chapter, we'll explore how to cultivate Right Effort in your daily life. Whether it's learning to shift away from frustration and burnout, replacing self-doubt with confidence, or simply finding the motivation to keep going, the way we train our minds shapes everything else—including how we approach work, relationships, and personal growth. Because when we put effort into creating peace within, we start to see that peace reflected in everything we do.

So, take a breath. Take a moment. And when you're ready, let's dive into the next step of this journey.

Chapter 9:
Cultivating a Positive Mindset (Right Effort—Samma Vayama)

You wake up to the sound of your alarm. Before your feet even hit the floor, your mind is already racing—thinking about emails, deadlines, that awkward conversation from yesterday, or your never-ending to-do list. The weight of the day presses down before it's even begun. It's automatic, almost like your brain has been trained to scan for problems before possibilities.

Now, what if I told you that Buddhism offers a simple, powerful way to break this cycle?

Enter Right Effort, one of the key teachings of the Eightfold Path. At its core, Right Effort is about mental discipline—not in a harsh, drill sergeant way, but in the way a gardener nurtures a garden. It's about choosing which thoughts to water and which to gently weed out (Lama Karma Yeshe Chödrön, 2023).

Buddha understood something that modern neuroscience confirms: What we focus on grows. If we constantly feed fear, doubt, and negativity, they flourish. But if we consciously nurture joy, patience, and kindness, they take root and change our inner landscape. Right Effort is the practice of tending to our minds with intention.

This isn't about toxic positivity—forcing yourself to be happy when you're struggling. It's about developing the skill of noticing unhelpful thoughts before they take over and making small, consistent choices to shift your focus toward more helpful, uplifting ones. Right Effort is about training yourself to meet challenges with resilience rather than getting stuck in suffering.

In this chapter, we'll explore how you can build a positive mindset through small, daily efforts that have both immediate and long-term benefits.

Buddhism reminds us that we're not powerless over our minds. Just as we wouldn't expect a neglected garden to bloom overnight, we don't need to master this in a single day. But with consistent, patient effort, we can gradually cultivate a mind that's more peaceful, resilient, and open to joy—no matter what life throws our way.

Let's begin.

Replacing Negative Thoughts With Positive Reflections

If you've ever caught yourself spiraling into a loop of negative thoughts—worrying about the future, replaying past mistakes, or just feeling stuck in self-doubt—you're not alone. Our minds have a tendency to lean toward the negative, a leftover survival mechanism from our ancestors who needed to be hyperaware of threats. But in our daily lives, this negativity bias often does more harm than good, keeping us trapped in patterns of stress, anxiety, and self-criticism.

I'm here to tell you that you don't have to be at the mercy of your thoughts. Right Effort teaches us that just as we can replace unhealthy habits with healthier ones, we can also replace negative thoughts with more positive and constructive reflections. You don't have to "just think happy thoughts," but you can learn how to shift your perspective in a way that actually supports your well-being.

Cognitive Restructuring: Rewiring the Way You Think

Think of your mind like a well-worn hiking trail. If you've been walking the same negative path for years, of course it feels automatic. But you have the power to carve a new trail—a more helpful, supportive one. Cognitive restructuring is the practice of identifying and challenging negative thoughts, then actively choosing more beneficial ones. You can get started by trying the following:

- **Notice the pattern:** Next time you catch yourself thinking, *I'll never get this right,* pause. Is that 100% true? Or is it just an old story your brain is telling you?

- **Reframe it:** Instead of, *I always fail,* try, *I'm still learning, and I've made progress before.*

- **Embrace the shift:** Recognizing and challenging harmful thinking patterns isn't just about feeling better in the moment—it's about long-term personal growth. Each time you interrupt a negative thought, you strengthen your ability to think in a more balanced and constructive way.

Affirmations and Visualizations: Training Your Mind for Positivity

Affirmations aren't just feel-good phrases you whisper to yourself in the mirror. They're powerful tools for rewiring your brain, helping to shift your subconscious beliefs and build confidence over time. The key is repetition and belief. Try the following:

- **Start small:** Choose affirmations that feel authentic and attainable (e.g., "I am capable of growth" instead of "I am the best in the world").

- **Make it a habit:** Repeat them daily—while brushing your teeth, commuting, or before bed.

- **Pair them with visualization:** Close your eyes and imagine yourself succeeding, feeling joyful, or being at peace. Your brain responds to visual cues, making these images more likely to become reality.

Over time, affirmations and visualizations reshape your inner dialogue, helping you approach challenges with a more empowered mindset.

Mindful Thinking: Becoming an Observer of Your Thoughts

Most of the time, we don't even realize how much negative thinking runs in the background. That's where mindfulness comes in—not to force positivity, but to cultivate awareness without judgment. You should consider

- observing your thoughts like passing clouds. You don't have to react to every one—just notice them and let them go.

- detaching from negativity. Instead of getting caught in the storm of self-criticism, practice saying, "Oh, that's just an old fear talking" and move on.

- showing yourself compassion. Treat your own thoughts the way you would a friend's—respond with understanding, not harshness.

When you stop fighting negative thoughts and simply watch them without attachment, they lose their power over you.

Gratitude Journaling: Redirecting Your Focus Toward the Good

If you train your mind to focus on what's wrong, that's all you'll see. But if you shift your attention to what's going right—no matter how small—it changes your entire perspective. You can try

- writing down three things you're grateful for each day. They don't have to be life-changing—just small joys, like a good conversation, a warm cup of tea, or a sunny morning.

- focusing on positive experiences. Instead of replaying a stressful moment, reflect on something uplifting from your day.

- making it a ritual. Whether it's morning or night, find a time that works for you. Consistency strengthens the practice.

Gratitude isn't about ignoring life's challenges—it's about reminding yourself that there's always light, even in difficult times. The more you train your brain to see the good, the more naturally it happens.

You Have More Power Over Your Mind Than You Think

Buddhism teaches us that we are not our thoughts—we are the ones who observe them. When you practice cognitive restructuring, affirmations, mindfulness, and gratitude, you can gradually shift from a mindset dominated by negativity to one that welcomes possibility, resilience, and peace.

Change takes time. But every time you choose a positive reflection over a negative spiral, you're rewiring your mind for a more joyful and fulfilling life. And that's a journey worth taking.

Let's continue.

Developing Proactive Gratitude Practices

Gratitude isn't just a feeling—it's a practice. And like any practice, the more you engage in it, the more natural it becomes. But it's easy to feel grateful when things are going well, right? The real challenge is building gratitude as a habit, something you can lean on even when life feels overwhelming.

In Buddhism, gratitude is more than just saying "thank you." It's about shifting our focus from what's missing to what's present, from what's wrong to what's right. This doesn't mean ignoring pain or struggles but rather training your mind to recognize joy, beauty, and kindness even in small moments. When you actively work on building gratitude, you create a powerful mindset shift—one that creates resilience, deepens relationships, and brings a greater sense of peace.

Daily Gratitude Rituals: Making Gratitude a Habit

Have you ever noticed how easy it is to get stuck in what's going wrong? The mind naturally latches on to problems, but gratitude helps redirect your focus. Keep being consistent, and you'll turn gratitude into a daily ritual rather than something you only think about on special occasions. You can accomplish this by doing the following:

- **Morning gratitude check-in:** Before you even get out of bed, take a moment to think of one thing you're grateful for. It could be as simple as having a cozy blanket, the warm cup of coffee waiting for you, or the fact that you woke up breathing.

- **Evening reflection:** Before bed, write down three things that brought you joy or comfort that day. Big or small, it all counts.

- **Gratitude reminders:** Set a phone alert, use sticky notes, or create a gratitude jar where you write something you appreciate every day. These tiny efforts train your brain to seek out the good, reshaping your mindset over time.

The more you practice gratitude intentionally, the more it becomes your default setting, leading to a more fulfilling and content life.

Sharing Gratitude: Strengthening Relationships Through Appreciation

Gratitude doesn't just benefit you—it strengthens your connections with others. Think about a time when someone genuinely appreciated you. Didn't it feel good? Now imagine if you became the source of that feeling for others:

- **Say it out loud.** Instead of keeping your appreciation to yourself, tell people when they've made a difference. A simple "I really appreciate how you always check in on me" can deepen a relationship instantly.

- **Write gratitude letters.** Take a few minutes to send a thoughtful text or handwritten note. It doesn't have to be long—just authentic.

- **Express gratitude in the workplace.** Recognizing your coworkers' efforts fosters mutual respect and strengthens teamwork. A culture of gratitude transforms work environments from draining to fulfilling.

When you make expressing gratitude a habit, you're not just improving your relationships—you're creating a ripple effect of positivity in your world.

Gratitude Challenges: Amplifying Gratitude Through Community

Gratitude can be contagious. When we practice it together, it grows even stronger. That's where gratitude challenges come in—group efforts to encourage a mindset shift and accountability. Here are some great ideas to consider:

- **Thirty-day gratitude challenge:** Each day, write down or share something you're grateful for. Seeing what others appreciate expands your own perspective.

- **Gratitude swap:** Partner with a friend or family member and send each other a quick text or voice message about one good thing each day. It keeps you both motivated and accountable.

- **Workplace gratitude boards:** Encourage colleagues to leave notes of appreciation for each other—small efforts like this can transform team dynamics and boost morale.

When gratitude is shared, it multiplies—making it easier to sustain even when life gets tough.

Visualizing Gratitude: Imagining a Life Rooted in Appreciation

The mind is powerful—what we focus on shapes our reality. When you visualize gratitude, you're not just imagining a better life; you're rewiring your brain to experience joy more deeply. Consider the following:

- **Morning gratitude meditation:** Close your eyes and picture a life where you're fully aware of and grateful for the little things—relationships, health, small daily comforts.

- **Future gratitude journaling:** Write as if you're already living the life you want: "I'm so grateful for the peace I feel every day, for the meaningful connections I've built, and for the way I handle challenges with grace." This trains your brain to seek out these experiences in real life.

- **Gratitude visualization in tough times:** When things feel overwhelming, visualize the support, love, and lessons that exist even in difficulty.

When you regularly envision a life filled with gratitude, it becomes easier to actually live that way.

Through daily rituals, sharing appreciation, engaging in gratitude challenges, and visualizing the life you want, you train your mind to focus on abundance instead of lack. And when that happens, life starts to feel lighter, richer, and more meaningful—not because your circumstances have changed, but because you have.

Final Thoughts

If there's one thing to take away from this chapter, it's this: Your mind isn't set in stone. You aren't stuck with the thoughts, habits, or perspectives you've carried for years. With small, consistent shifts—whether it's replacing negative thoughts with positive reflections, developing gratitude practices, or simply observing your mind with more kindness—you can begin to cultivate a more peaceful, resilient, and joyful way of being.

You can't change a thought pattern if you don't notice it. You can't cultivate gratitude if you're too distracted to see what's already good. And you certainly can't shift your mindset if you're lost in autopilot. This is where Right Mindfulness comes in.

Mindfulness is what makes all of these changes possible. It's what allows you to pause before reacting, notice before spiraling, and choose before getting caught up in the same old patterns. It's about learning to be fully present—not just in the quiet, peaceful moments but in the messy, ordinary, frustrating ones, too.

In the next chapter, we'll explore how to deepen your awareness of your body, feelings, and thoughts through the practice of mindfulness. Because once you truly start paying attention, you'll realize just how much power you have to shift your experience—not by changing the world around you, but by changing the way you meet it.

Chapter 10:
Awakening to the Present Moment (Right Mindfulness—Samma Sati)

Imagine standing on a beach, watching waves roll in and out. For a few moments, you're not thinking about that email you forgot to send, what's for dinner, or the million other thoughts pulling you in every direction. You're just there, fully present with the sound of the waves, the salty breeze, and the warmth of the sun on your skin. That feeling—that deep sense of simply being—is what Right Mindfulness is all about.

In Buddhism, Right Mindfulness is a core part of the Eightfold Path and is often described as the heart of mindful living. It's about waking up to the present moment, not as we wish it to be but exactly as it is (Huxter, n.d.-b). That might sound simple, but in our fast-paced, endlessly scrolling world, being truly present can feel like an impossible task. Our minds jump from one thought to another like monkeys swinging through trees—what Buddhists call the "monkey mind." Right Mindfulness teaches us how to gently guide that monkey back to the here and now.

This chapter is an invitation to slow down and connect with yourself—your body, your feelings, your thoughts—without judgment or the urge to fix anything. It's not about reaching some perfect state of zen. It's about cultivating awareness so you can experience life more fully, with greater clarity and compassion.

We'll explore simple practices to help you develop mindfulness in your everyday life—whether you're brushing your teeth, walking the dog, or sitting in traffic. We'll look at how tuning into your body can help you spot tension and stress before they take over, how noticing your feelings can lead to emotional balance, and how observing your thoughts can free you from patterns that no longer serve you.

Right Mindfulness doesn't expect you to empty your mind. It focuses on noticing what's happening right now, in this very moment, and understanding that this awareness is where real change begins. With patience and consistency, mindfulness can transform how you relate to yourself, others, and the world around you—offering more peace, clarity, and joy in the process.

So, let's take a deep breath together. Inhale. Exhale. And let's begin this journey of awakening to the present moment.

Observing Bodily Sensations and Feelings

How does your body react when you're stressed or anxious? Maybe your shoulders tighten, your jaw clenches, or your stomach knots up like a pretzel. Or, on the flip side, think about how your body feels when you're relaxed and content—your breathing slows, your muscles soften, and everything just feels... lighter. Our bodies are constantly sending us messages, but in the chaos of daily life, we often forget to listen.

This is where the practice of observing bodily sensations and feelings comes in. It's about tuning into your body—noticing that racing heartbeat, that flutter in your stomach, or even that subtle tension in your forehead. And it's not just about the physical stuff. Our emotions live in our bodies too. Becoming more aware of these sensations allows us to ground ourselves in the present moment and start to understand the beautiful (and sometimes messy) connection between our body and mind.

Understanding the Connection: Your Body Talks—Are You Listening?

Our bodies are like mirrors reflecting our emotional states. That headache? It could be stress. The warm, open feeling spreading through your body? Maybe it's joy. When we pay attention to these signals, we start to recognize how closely our physical sensations and emotions are intertwined.

This kind of holistic awareness helps us become more attuned to ourselves. It's like having a road map that shows us where we're holding on to stress or where we're feeling free and open. And when life gets overwhelming (because it will), simply grounding ourselves in these sensations can be a powerful anchor. It gives us something solid to hold on to in the storm.

Another perk? Noticing shifts in your body can offer insights into emotional triggers. That sudden tightness in your stomach during a meeting? Maybe it's not just the bad coffee—it could be a subtle sign of anxiety or frustration. Becoming aware of these shifts lets you explore what's going on beneath the surface, helping you respond more thoughtfully rather than reacting on autopilot.

Breath Awareness: Your Built-In Reset Button

If bodily sensations are like messages, your breath is the delivery system—and it's always with you. Focusing on your breath is one of the simplest and most effective ways to ground yourself in the present moment. It's like having a portable mindfulness tool you can use anytime, anywhere.

When you pay attention to your breathing, you create space between yourself and the chaos around you. Just noticing the inhale and exhale—without trying to change anything—can calm a racing mind and ease tension. In moments of stress, a few deep, conscious breaths can feel like hitting the reset button.

Practicing mindful breathing also helps in softening difficult emotions. Say you're feeling overwhelmed. Instead of getting swept away by the feeling, you can pause, focus on your breath, and create a little room around the emotion. This doesn't make the feeling disappear, but it gives you the space to observe it with kindness and curiosity rather than judgment.

Emotional Check-Ins: How Are You Really Feeling?

When was the last time you stopped to ask yourself, "How am I feeling right now?" Not in a way that accepts the autopilot "I'm fine" response, but a real check-in. Emotional check-ins are a simple yet powerful way to reconnect with yourself. They're like little pit stops during the day that let you assess where you're at, both emotionally and physically.

These check-ins don't have to be complicated. It could be as simple as pausing while waiting for your coffee to brew and asking, "What's going on inside me right now?" Maybe you notice a flutter of anxiety, a sense of calm, or even just a feeling of boredom. The key is to notice without judgment. There's no right or wrong way to feel.

Over time, these emotional check-ins can help you build emotional intelligence. Tuning into your feelings lets you become better equipped to respond to emotions instead of reacting impulsively. That means fewer knee-jerk reactions and more thoughtful interactions—with yourself and with others.

Bringing awareness to your bodily sensations and emotions isn't intended to make you start overanalyzing or fixing anything. The focus is on gently waking up to what's already happening inside you. With practice, this awareness becomes a steady, grounding force you can return to, no matter what life throws your way. And in that stillness, you might just discover a deeper connection to yourself and the present moment.

Deepening Present-Moment Awareness

We live in a world that seems to thrive on distraction. Our phones buzz with notifications, our to-do lists never end, and somehow, we've all become experts at eating lunch while answering emails and scrolling social media—all at the same time. It's no wonder we often feel frazzled, disconnected, and a little bit like we're living on autopilot. But the peace we're chasing isn't somewhere out there, waiting for us to find it. It's right here, in this very moment—we just have to learn how to notice it.

Let's explore how simple, mindful moments can help you reconnect with the present—no meditation cushion required.

Mindful Eating: Savor Every Bite

When was the last time you really tasted your food? As in, noticed the flavors, textures, and aromas without also binge-watching a show or mindlessly scrolling through your phone, then looking down and wondering how your plate is empty? Mindful eating invites you to slow down and fully engage during mealtimes, turning something you do every day into a grounding and joyful practice.

The point isn't to count every bite. The goal is to create a healthier, more conscious relationship with food. When you pay attention to the colors on your plate, the aroma wafting up, the crunch of that first bite, or the way flavors blend together, something amazing happens: You start to enjoy your food more, often feeling fuller and more satisfied with less.

This practice also helps disrupt the cycle of mindless eating—you know, when you look down and realize you've demolished an entire bag of chips without tasting a single one. By tuning in, you give yourself a chance to notice your body's hunger and fullness cues and maybe even foster a little gratitude for the food in front of you. Even one mindful meal a day can be transformative.

Nature Connection: Finding Stillness in the Great Outdoors

If you've ever taken a deep breath while standing under a canopy of trees or felt instantly calmer watching waves crash on the shore, you already know the magic of connecting with nature. There's something about the natural world that pulls us into the present moment—it invites us to pause, notice, and just be.

Maybe you're reading this and saying, "I don't have time for weekend hiking trips." I get it. But even a short walk through a park, sitting by a tree, or tending to a houseplant can help ground you. Try slowing down and noticing the small details—the intricate patterns on a leaf, the sound of birdsong, or how the sunlight filters through the trees. Me? I love putting my bare feet in the grass in my backyard. We did this all the time as children, yet as adults, our first instinct is to throw on our shoes. Give it a try and reconnect to nature.

Studies continue to show us that this kind of mindful connection with nature reduces stress and creates a sense of wonder and gratitude (Djernis et al., 2019). It reminds us that we're part of something bigger—a living, breathing world that's constantly unfolding in the present moment.

Everyday Mindfulness: Turning the Mundane Into the Meaningful

One of the biggest misconceptions about mindfulness is that it only happens when you're sitting in meditation, legs crossed, eyes closed. But some of the most powerful mindful moments come from the simplest daily routines. Walking to the store, washing dishes, folding laundry—these can all become opportunities to practice present-moment awareness.

The key? Bring your full attention to the task at hand. Feel the warm water as you wash the dishes, notice the sensation of your feet hitting the pavement as you walk, or pay attention to the rhythm of your breath while stuck in traffic. They might sound small, but these moments add up. Over time, infusing mindfulness into your daily activities strengthens your resilience against distractions and brings a sense of calm into the everyday.

Plus, there's something beautiful about finding peace in the ordinary. It's like discovering that life's little moments—the ones we often rush through—are where the real magic happens.

Mindfulness Techniques for Busy Lives: Quick Practices With Big Impact

"I don't have time for mindfulness." Sound familiar? Trust me, I get it. Life is busy. But mindfulness doesn't have to mean carving out hours of your day. Even a few mindful moments sprinkled throughout your schedule can make a big difference.

Here are some simple, effective techniques you can practice anytime, anywhere:

- **One-minute breather:** Pause what you're doing and take slow, deep breaths for one minute. Focus on the sensation of the air moving in and out. It's like a mini reset for your mind.

- **Sensory check-in:** Wherever you are, pause and notice five things you can see, four you can touch, three you can hear, two you can smell, and one you can taste. It's a grounding exercise that pulls you right into the moment.

- **Mindful pauses:** Before answering an email or jumping into your next task, pause and take a deep breath. Take a sip of cold water. These tiny breaks help interrupt the constant flow of busyness and create space for presence.

- **Gratitude moments:** While waiting in line or commuting, think of three things you're grateful for. It's a simple way to shift your mindset and connect with the present.

The beauty of these practices is that they fit into your existing life—they don't require special equipment or extra time. And over time, even these small moments of mindfulness can lead to big shifts: less stress, more focus, and a deeper sense of peace, right in the middle of your wonderfully messy, busy life.

Deepening your present-moment awareness isn't about being perfect or living every second in mindful bliss, because that's not realistic. It's about creating more moments—small but meaningful—

where you're fully here. And in those moments, you'll discover a calmer mind, a fuller heart, and the simple, grounding peace that comes from being present with life as it is.

Final Thoughts

You've explored what it means to truly wake up to the present moment. We've talked about how Right Mindfulness doesn't focus on achieving some kind of perfect stillness or clearing your mind of every thought (because, seriously, who can actually do that?). It centers on showing up for your life, moment by moment, with curiosity, compassion, and maybe even a little bit of gratitude.

You've learned how observing your bodily sensations and emotions can act as an anchor, bringing you back when your mind starts racing or when life feels overwhelming. You've discovered how simple acts like breathing deeply, savoring a bite of food, or noticing the way the sunlight is filtering through the trees can ground you in the here and now. And you've seen that mindfulness doesn't require a mountain retreat or hours of free time. It's something you can weave into the tiniest corners of your day—during your morning coffee, on a walk to the mailbox, or even while brushing your teeth.

Remember, mindfulness is a practice. And, like any practice, it comes with its good days and not-so-great days. Some moments will feel effortless and peaceful, and others… well, you might feel like you're herding cats. That's okay. You don't have to get it right—you just have to keep showing up again and again, with patience and kindness toward yourself.

And now that you've built this beautiful foundation of awareness, it's time to take it a step further.

In the next chapter, we'll dive into Right Concentration—the art of sharpening the mind. If mindfulness is about noticing the present moment, concentration is about focusing deeply, like when you're so absorbed in something that the rest of the world seems to disappear. It's where you move from simply being aware to building a steadier, calmer mind—one that doesn't get yanked around by every passing thought.

So, take a deep breath. Let it out slowly.

You're already on the path. Let's keep going—together.

Chapter 11:
Sharpening the Mind (Right Concentration—Samma Samadhi)

I want you to picture your mind as a glass of water filled with dirt and sand. When stirred, the water becomes cloudy, making it hard to see through. But if you let the glass sit still, the dirt settles at the bottom and the water becomes clear again. That's exactly what Right Concentration is about—allowing the chaos in our minds to settle so we can see clearly.

In the whirlwind of modern life—nonstop expectations, endless to-do lists, and the pressure to always be on—it's easy for our minds to feel stirred up all the time. Focus becomes fragmented and clarity feels like a distant dream. But Buddhism offers us a tool to still the waters: Right Concentration, the eighth step on the Noble Eightfold Path.

Right Concentration is the practice of deep meditation, cultivating focus and calm. It's not about striving for a perfect, blank mind. It's about learning to gently guide your attention, again and again, to a single point of focus, allowing mental clutter to drift away. In this space, clarity, calm, and insight can naturally arise.

This chapter will guide you through the essence of Right Concentration—what it really means, why it changes everything for mental clarity, and how you can start practicing it today. We'll explore simple, realistic techniques to strengthen your focus, even if you only have five minutes between meetings or while waiting in the carpool line.

The beauty of Right Concentration is that it meets you where you are. Whether you're brand new to meditation or you've dabbled here and there, this practice can help you sharpen your mind, reduce overwhelm, and experience moments of peace in the chaos. It's not about achieving some mystical state; it's about making space for your mind to breathe and find stillness amid the noise.

Like anything worth doing, building concentration takes patience, consistency, and self-kindness. Think of it as a gentle strengthening of your mind's muscles.

By the end of this chapter, you'll have tools and techniques to start sharpening your mind, creating moments of clarity that ripple into every part of your life. Whether you're looking to be more present with your family, less reactive at work, or simply more at peace within yourself, Right Concentration offers a path to get there.

Focusing on a Single Object: The Gentle Art of Anchoring the Mind

Our minds have a knack for wandering. One moment you're deep in your breath, and the next you're planning dinner, replaying yesterday's chat, or worrying if that email came across too harshly. It's totally normal. Our thoughts resemble playful puppies—curious, eager, and constantly darting off in different directions. The wonderful thing about meditation, especially when practicing Right Concentration, is that it teaches us to gently steer our busy minds back to a single point of focus again and again.

This is where the art of concentrating on a single object comes into play. It may sound simple, but it's profoundly transformative.

Choosing Your Object: Finding Your Anchor

Think of your meditation object as an anchor in a stormy sea. When thoughts, emotions, and outside noise swirl around you, your anchor keeps you steady. It could be something as simple as your breath—the gentle rise and fall of your chest—or the soft glow of a candle flame. Some people prefer focusing on a soothing sound, like the hum of a fan or a particular mantra.

Choosing your object is about discovering what feels natural and supportive to you. There's no right or wrong choice; what matters is finding something that gives your mind a gentle place to land. With time, focusing on this single point of concentration strengthens your mental muscles, allowing distractions to settle like dust in a still room. The more you return to this object, the deeper your meditation gets, just like diving into the calm waters beneath the choppy surface.

Techniques for Sustaining Focus: Keeping Your Mind Engaged

Even with the perfect anchor, your mind will wander—that's all part of the process. But there are techniques to help you maintain your focus and make the experience feel more grounded.

One easy method is counting your breaths. Inhale—one. Exhale—two. Go up to ten, then start over. If you lose count (and you will), gently return to one. This gives your mind a task, helping you stay connected to the present moment.

Another technique is visualization. Imagine your breath as a soft light moving through your body, or picture yourself by a peaceful stream, with each thought drifting past like leaves on the water. Visualization can engage the mind more actively, which is helpful if you enjoy imagery.

The key here is flexibility. Experiment with different methods and see what feels right for you. There's no one-size-fits-all approach— these techniques are tools to help your mind settle, giving you more moments of clarity amid the usual chaos.

Overcoming Distractions: Gentle Redirection

Distractions are a given. Thoughts will pop up: *Did I send that email? What's for dinner? Why is my leg itchy?* The goal isn't to chase these thoughts away but to acknowledge them gently, without judgment, and then redirect your focus back to your chosen object.

Picture your wandering mind like a child learning to walk. It stumbles and gets distracted, veering off course—but with gentle encouragement, it returns. Each time you recognize a distraction and come back to your breath (or candle, or sound), you're strengthening your focus. It's like a workout at the gym but for your mind.

Patience is crucial here. No scolding or frustration—just gentle redirection. Over time, this practice builds not only concentration but also resilience. You'll find it easier to return to focus, both during meditation and in your everyday life.

Creating a Regular Practice: Building Your Focus Muscle

The magic formula for deepening your concentration? Consistency. It's not about meditating for an hour once a week; it's about showing up daily, even if it's just for five minutes. Think of it like watering a plant—it needs regular care to grow.

Set aside a specific time each day, whether it's first thing in the morning or right before bed. Even brief sessions, done consistently, can lead to profound changes. Over time, this practice becomes a thread woven through the fabric of your life, creating moments of calm amid the busyness.

And keep in mind that perfection isn't the goal. Some days, your focus will feel as sharp as a tack; other days, it might feel all over the place. Both experiences are valid. The real essence of this practice is to show up, sit down, and return to your chosen object, time and again.

By focusing on a single object during meditation, you're not just honing your concentration—you're cultivating clarity, patience, and resilience. It's a gentle yet powerful act of self-care. Over time, this practice seeps into your daily life. Conversations become more present. Tasks feel less daunting. Your once-scattered mind starts to resemble a clear glass of water—calm, focused, and at peace.

And isn't that a beautiful gift to give yourself?

Improving Concentration Through Sustained Practices: Building Focus Over Time

Think of concentration like a muscle—the more you work on it, the stronger it gets. Just like at the gym, you don't start with the heaviest weights. You begin where you are and gradually increase the challenge as your strength grows. Improving your focus through sustained meditation practices is a gentle journey of growth that rewards consistency and patience rather than providing quick results.

Sharpening your mind with meditation isn't about forcing stillness or chasing perfection. It's about committing to showing up day after day, allowing your ability to focus to expand naturally. This section discusses how sustained practices can deepen your concentration over time, providing tools and approaches to keep you engaged in your journey.

Progressive Meditation Sessions: Growing Your Practice Step by Step

When you first start meditating, even five minutes can feel like forever. Thoughts race, fidgeting kicks in, and the urge to check your phone is strong—that's completely normal. The key is to start small and gradually increase your meditation time.

Begin with short, manageable sessions—maybe five to ten minutes. Once that feels comfortable, gently extend it to fifteen minutes, then twenty minutes, and so on. This slow approach allows your mind to adapt, building its tolerance for stillness and focus—much like increasing your stamina during workouts.

Longer sessions introduce new layers to your practice. You'll likely face more distractions, moments of boredom, or unexpected insights. While these experiences can be challenging, they cultivate patience and persistence, teaching you to sit with discomfort and consistently return to your point of focus.

Extended sessions also help your mind to settle more deeply. The longer you sit, the more your thoughts can soften, like ripples on a pond slowly calming down. Over time, you'll start to notice moments of genuine stillness—fleeting at first, but increasingly accessible the more you practice.

Periodic Reflection: Understanding Your Meditation Journey

When we focus on where we want to go, we often forget how far we've come. This is where reflection can become an invaluable tool in your meditation practice.

Taking time to reflect on your meditation experiences—whether through journaling, voice notes, or simply sitting quietly—can provide you with profound insights into your progress. Ask yourself: "What felt easy today? What pulled my attention away? Did I notice any shifts in my focus or mood afterward?" These simple questions can reveal patterns in your practice and highlight areas of growth.

There's no need for formal or complicated record-keeping. Even jotting down a few thoughts after each session can create a meaningful log of your journey. With time, you'll look back and see how your concentration has strengthened, even on days that felt tough.

Reflection also helps you recognize personal roadblocks. Maybe you notice certain thoughts that consistently distract you, or that some days feel harder than others. Rather than viewing these as failures, use reflection as an opportunity: "What can I learn from this?" This gentle curiosity keeps your practice engaged and evolving.

Engaging With Community: Finding Support on the Path

Meditation may seem like a solitary practice, but there's immense power in sharing the journey with others. Whether it's joining a group meditation, taking a class, or connecting online, engaging with a community can be powerful.

Practicing with others creates a shared energy—a kind of collective stillness that can deepen your own focus. It's like hiking with friends; while the path may be challenging, the company makes it more manageable and enjoyable.

Community also brings accountability and motivation. Knowing that others are meditating alongside you, even virtually, can encourage you to show up on days when you might otherwise skip. Connecting with fellow meditators can also introduce you to new techniques or perspectives that enhance your practice.

Perhaps most importantly, community provides support during tough times. Meditation isn't always easy, and it's reassuring to know you're not alone in the struggle to quiet a restless mind. Sharing experiences, asking questions, or simply listening to others can create a sense of connection that keeps you grounded and inspired.

The Beauty of Sustained Practice

Improving concentration through meditation isn't about quick fixes or overnight results—it's a gradual unfolding. Through progressive sessions, regular reflection, and community support, you're cultivating a skill that sharpens your focus and enriches every aspect of your life.

You'll begin to notice it in everyday moments—like staying present during conversations, focusing on tasks without constant distractions, or simply sitting in stillness without restlessness. These shifts may seem subtle, but over time, they create profound changes in how you experience the world.

Remember, this is your personal practice. There's no right timeline or perfect method. The goal isn't to master your mind but to foster a kind and consistent relationship with it. With patience, reflection, and perhaps a little support from a community, your concentration will deepen, bringing more clarity and calm into your life—one mindful breath at a time.

Final Thoughts

As we wrap up this chapter on sharpening the mind and cultivating Right Concentration, take a moment to acknowledge the journey you've undertaken. You've learned to anchor your focus, gently guide your attention back when it drifts, and nurture your mind's capacity for clarity through sustained practice. With each breath and each moment of stillness, you've been polishing the surface of a mirror—slowly allowing your true reflection to shine.

But here's the beautiful paradox: As your focus sharpens, something else begins to soften—the tight grip of identity and the persistent voice whispering, "I am this" or "I am not that." In the spaces between thoughts, during those quiet moments of stillness, you may have glimpsed something deeper—a sense of peace that isn't tied to any label, achievement, or role.

This leads us naturally to the next step on this path: letting go of the ego—or, in Buddhist philosophy, embracing *anatta*, the concept of "no-self."

It might seem a bit abstract to start with—the notion that the "self" we cling to is more like passing clouds than a solid, unchanging entity. But letting go of the ego isn't about losing ourselves or denying our uniqueness. It's about releasing the stories we tell ourselves—the ones that limit us, confine us, and sometimes bring us pain.

In the next chapter, we'll explore what it means to gently loosen the grip of the ego. We'll dive into how the mind constructs identity and how this sense of "I" can lead to struggle and separation. Together, we'll discover practices that help soften the boundaries between self and others, allowing you to move through life with more compassion, ease, and freedom.

Consider this: As you've learned to focus your mind, you've also paved the way for a quiet, open space where thoughts come and go without sticking. What if the same could apply to your sense of self? What if, by letting go just a little, you could experience life with more fluidity, connection, and peace?

As we journey into the next chapter, carry with you the stillness you've created here. Let it serve as a gentle landing as we explore the art of releasing the ego—not as an act of loss but as a liberating return to your true, expansive nature.

Chapter 12:
Letting Go of the Ego (Anatta)

What if I told you that the person you think you are—the one with all the labels, roles, and stories—might not be as solid or fixed as you believe? Sounds a little wild, right? But this is at the heart of a core Buddhist principle called *anatta*, or "no-self." It's not about denying your existence or becoming some kind of blank slate. It's about loosening your grip on who you think you are and, in doing so, finding a freedom you might not have realized was possible.

In today's world, the idea of "me, myself, and I" is everywhere. We're constantly encouraged to define ourselves—through our jobs, our achievements, our social media profiles, even the kind of coffee we drink. And while there's nothing wrong with having preferences or goals, the problem arises when we start to believe that these things are all we are. That's when the ego takes the wheel and life can start to feel heavy, competitive, and, let's be honest, a bit exhausting.

The Buddhist principle of *anatta* invites us to step back from that constant identity-building project. It's like being able to take off a heavy backpack we didn't even realize we were carrying. When we let go of our tight grip on ego—on the stories that say "I am this" or "I am not that"—we open up to a deeper, more peaceful way of being.

Now, this isn't about suddenly becoming egoless (if that were even possible). It's about noticing when the ego is running the show and gently inviting it to take a back seat. In this chapter, we're going to explore what *anatta* really means in a simple, everyday way. We'll look at how the ego shows up in our lives through roles, reactions, and the need to be right or special. And, most importantly, I'll walk you through a few practices that can help you soften that attachment, creating more space for peace, compassion, and freedom.

The beautiful thing about this practice is that it's about showing up, noticing, and letting go—again and again—with kindness and patience. And the benefits? A lighter heart, deeper connections with others, and a growing sense that maybe, just maybe, you don't have to hold on so tightly after all.

Meditating on the Impermanence of Self

Let's talk about something we all experience but rarely question—our thoughts. They come and go all day long, like clouds drifting across the sky. Some are light and fluffy (*What should I have for lunch?*) while others are heavy and stormy (*I'll never be good enough*). But if thoughts are so fleeting, constantly changing from one moment to the next, how can they define who we are?

This is where meditating on the impermanence of self becomes a powerful tool. In Buddhism, this idea connects deeply with *anatta*—the principle of no-self. It asks us to notice that who we think we are isn't as fixed as we believe. Our identities, like our thoughts, are in constant motion. And that's not a bad thing—it's actually liberating.

Think about it: How often do you catch yourself stuck in an identity shaped by a single thought? *I'm so disorganized* or *I'm not good at relationships*—these thoughts might feel true in the moment, but are they really who you are? If you sit with it, you can start to see that these ideas about yourself are just passing through. They don't have to define you unless you let them.

When you meditate on the impermanence of self, you start to see your thoughts for what they are—temporary, shifting, and often unreliable. It's like observing clouds drift across the sky. Some captivate your gaze while others pass by without a glance, but none of them *are* the sky. In the same way, your thoughts are not *you*.

This realization can be incredibly freeing. It helps untangle the tight knots of self-identification that often lead to anxiety and self-criticism. When we stop clinging to every passing thought as proof of who we are, we create space for self-compassion and growth. We're no longer boxed in by old narratives like "I'm just an anxious person" or "I'll never be successful." Instead, we begin to see ourselves as people who, like everything else in life, are fluid and ever-changing.

This mindset opens the door to growth. When you understand that your identity isn't set in stone, you give yourself permission to evolve. You're not chained to yesterday's mistakes or last week's self-doubt. Each moment becomes a chance to start fresh.

Meditating on impermanence can be as simple as pausing during a stressful moment and asking yourself, "Is this thought true? Will it still feel this big tomorrow?" That small gap between you and the thought is where freedom lives.

When you recognize the transient nature of self, you gently loosen your grip on the need to define who you are at every turn. And in that softening, you may just find a little more peace—and a lot more room to grow.

Shifting Relationships and Changing Emotions: Embracing the Flow of Life

Have you ever thought about how much you've changed in the last five years? Or how your relationships have shifted—some deepened, some faded, and others completely transformed? It's a little wild when you really sit with it. The people we're closest to, the roles we play, even the way we feel about ourselves—all of it is in constant motion. And just like our thoughts, our relationships and emotions remind us of one essential truth: Nothing stays the same forever.

Let's start with relationships. We often think of them as fixed—like once you're best friends, partners, or family, that bond will never change. But the reality? Relationships are more like rivers than statues. They flow, twist, deepen, or sometimes dry up altogether. And that's not necessarily a bad thing. In fact, it's part of what makes them beautiful.

When we understand that relationships are always evolving, it becomes easier to let go of the rigid ideas we attach to them—like how things should be or how they used to be. This shift helps us interpret changes with more compassion. A friendship that grows distant doesn't have to be a failure. A romantic relationship that changes form doesn't mean it's lost its value. These shifts are simply reflections of life's natural flow.

And here's the liberating part: When we stop clinging to the idea that relationships need to stay the same to be meaningful, we open ourselves up to continual renewal. Instead of fearing loss or change, we begin to value the now. We appreciate the present moment in a relationship, knowing that it's part of an ever-moving current. This awareness builds deeper, more mindful connections—because we're no longer stuck in the past or anxious about the future. We're here, now, appreciating the relationship as it is in this very moment.

Changing Emotions

Now, let's talk emotions. We can agree that some are lovely, some are messy, and others show up way too often. But no matter how intense they feel, they all have one thing in common: They come and go.

It's easy to forget this when we're in the middle of a big emotional wave—whether it's overwhelming sadness, blinding anger, or pure joy. In those moments, it feels like this is it: *This emotion defines me right now.* But emotions are like weather patterns—they roll in, sometimes without warning, and they eventually pass.

Recognizing this impermanence is powerful. It helps us avoid getting swept away by our feelings. When we realize that emotions are temporary, we're less likely to overidentify with them. You're not an "angry person" because you had a bad day. You're not "broken" because you feel lost. These are passing states, not permanent fixtures.

This understanding empowers us to seek emotional harmony rather than feeling trapped in the highs and lows. We learn to ride the emotional waves with more grace—embracing joy without clinging to it, and facing sadness without drowning in it. It's about finding that middle space where we can feel deeply but not be defined by those feelings.

And guess what? This builds resilience. When you acknowledge that your emotions are constantly shifting, you're less likely to fear them. The intense ones lose some of their power, and you become more grounded through the ups and downs.

Together, seeing the fluid nature of both relationships and emotions helps us loosen our grip on the fixed idea of self. If who we are is influenced by these shifting dynamics, then we're not stuck—we're evolving. And in that evolution, there's so much room for compassion, freedom, and connection.

Life's Ephemeral Nature: Embracing the Beauty of Impermanence

Life, in all its messy, beautiful, unpredictable glory, is fleeting. And while that can feel heavy at first—because, let's face it, the idea of impermanence often leads us straight to thoughts of death—it's also where some of the deepest wisdom in Buddhism lies.

The cycle of life and death is the ultimate reminder that everything changes. Flowers bloom and wither. Seasons come and go. People enter our lives and, eventually, they leave—sometimes gradually, sometimes suddenly. And yes, one day, we too will take our final breath.

Now, before this starts sounding too somber, let's pause and flip that perspective. Because here's the beautiful part: Knowing that life is ephemeral can actually be one of the most powerful invitations to live fully, deeply, and authentically.

When we recognize that time is limited—not in a panicky, "bucket list" kind of way, but in a gentle, mindful way—we start to see life differently. Small moments take on more significance. A sunrise becomes more than just the start of a new day; it's a gift, a fleeting piece of beauty that won't repeat itself in exactly the same way again. Conversations with loved ones feel richer. Even the mundane—washing dishes, walking the dog, sitting in traffic—can become moments of presence when we realize they're part of this one, precious life.

Embracing life's transience naturally cultivates gratitude. When we stop expecting everything (and everyone) to stick around forever, we start appreciating them for what they are—temporary, yes, but meaningful. Gratitude stops being something we practice only on holidays or after big events and starts becoming a daily habit. It's in the warm cup of coffee, the laughter of a friend, the sound of rain against the window.

This awareness also has a way of shifting our focus. We live in a world that often equates happiness with having more—more stuff, more achievements, more likes on a photo. But when we really sit with the impermanence of life, we realize that material things, while nice, aren't what truly fill us up. It's the experiences, the connections, the moments of genuine presence that leave lasting impressions on the heart.

And perhaps most importantly, embracing the ephemeral nature of life can help us live more authentically. When we understand that time is finite, we start questioning what truly matters. Are we living in alignment with our values? Are we spending our days doing things that bring us joy, connection, and purpose? Or are we stuck in cycles that don't serve us—clinging to relationships, jobs, or identities out of habit or fear?

Death, in this sense, isn't just an end—it's a teacher. It reminds us that life is precious *because* it's temporary. It encourages us to let go of the trivial and focus on what's real. It invites us to show up fully, to love deeply, and to live with a kind of raw, honest presence that's rare in a world obsessed with permanence.

So, while the truth of impermanence can be bittersweet, it's also where life's richest moments are born. It's the reason why a fleeting sunset can move us to tears or why a simple "I love you" can feel so profound. It's what makes life *life*—fragile, unpredictable, and utterly beautiful.

Reflections on the Changing Nature of Identity

Who are you? It sounds like a simple question, but when you sit with it for a moment, the answer gets a little blurry. Are you your job title? Your family role? Your beliefs, experiences, or dreams? The truth is, identity isn't some fixed label we slap on ourselves—it's more like a living, breathing collage of experiences, influences, and evolving perspectives.

Buddhism invites us to look deeply at this ever-changing nature of identity, not to make us feel untethered but to offer freedom. When we recognize that who we are isn't set in stone, we open the door to transformation, healing, and growth. Let's dive into how this plays out in our lives.

Past Experiences: You Are More Than Your Story

It's easy to fall into the trap of believing that our past defines us. Maybe it's a mistake we made, a relationship that ended badly, or a childhood wound that left a deep imprint. These experiences can feel like they've stamped us with a permanent label: "failure," "unlovable," "not enough." But your past is just part of your story, not the whole story.

Our identities are shaped by countless moments, both big and small, but they aren't frozen in time. Recognizing this gives us space to grow beyond old narratives. It means that the person who struggled with self-doubt 10 years ago isn't the same person reading this right now. We're constantly evolving, whether we notice it or not.

This realization opens pathways to personal change, growth, and healing. It allows us to hold our past with compassion, acknowledging it without letting it dictate our future. Understanding that identity is fluid creates self-acceptance, even during moments of change or uncertainty. It also empowers us to actively design our futures rather than feeling trapped by who we used to be.

Cultural and Social Influences: The Masks We Wear

We're all influenced by the world around us—whether we realize it or not. Our cultural backgrounds, societal norms, and even social media shape how we see ourselves and how we present ourselves to others. It's like we're wearing invisible masks that reflect what's expected of us. But just because these influences exist doesn't mean they have to define us.

Recognizing the cultural and social forces at play in shaping our identity gives us a powerful tool—the ability to choose. We can begin to discern which parts of ourselves feel authentic and which are simply echoes of societal expectations. This kind of awareness helps us make conscious choices about how we show up in the world.

And there's another gift here: When we see how much our identities are influenced by external forces, it becomes easier to accept diversity. We realize that everyone's self is a unique blend of experiences, shaped by different cultures, values, and environments. Instead of seeing differences as divisions, we start to view them as enriching aspects of the human experience.

Aging and Growth: Becoming Who You Already Are

Think about who you were at 18 versus who you are now. Odds are, you've gone through phases, shifts in perspective, and maybe even complete reinventions. Aging, in this sense, isn't just about getting older—it's about change.

In many ways, our identities flow through life stages, each one offering its own set of challenges and wisdom. Embracing this evolution invites us to view aging not as a decline but as a deepening. With each passing year, we gather insights, build resilience, and (hopefully) learn to let go of the things that no longer serve us.

Understanding the changing nature of identity can also help ease the fears often attached to aging. When we see life as a continual process of becoming rather than a march toward an endpoint, it's easier to appreciate the journey. Each stage brings new opportunities for growth, self-discovery, and connection.

The Freedom in Change

So, what does all this mean for you? It means that your identity isn't a box you're stuck in—it's a canvas you get to keep painting. It's a mix of your past, your present choices, and the limitless possibilities of your future.

By reflecting on the shifting nature of identity, we start to loosen the grip of rigid self-definitions. We make room for compassion—for ourselves and others. And we open up to the idea that who we are isn't something we need to "find" or "perfect." It's something we get to explore, shape, and, most importantly, live.

Final Thoughts

We've covered a lot together in this chapter—from the slippery nature of identity to the ever-changing tides of our thoughts, emotions, relationships, and even life itself. We explored how *anatta*, the Buddhist principle of no-self, invites us to loosen our grip on who we think we are and opens the door to living with more freedom, compassion, and presence. It's not about erasing ourselves or becoming detached robots—it's about recognizing that we're so much more fluid and expansive than the labels and stories we carry.

If there's one thing I hope you're walking away with, it's this: You're not stuck. Your past doesn't define you. Your roles, your thoughts, even your emotions—they're all part of your story, but they don't sum you up. There's a vast, peaceful space underneath all that chatter, and Buddhism gently points you there—not through force or perfection but through mindful awareness and kindness toward yourself.

Understanding these ideas is one thing; actually living them is another. You might have read about impermanence and thought, *Yes! This makes so much sense!*—only to find yourself, five minutes later, spiraling into self-doubt over a passing thought or clinging tightly to an old grudge. That's normal. That's the practice.

And that brings us to where we're headed next.

In the upcoming chapter, we're going to dive into something super important—overcoming challenges in Buddhist practice. Because implementing these principles into daily life isn't always smooth sailing. Maybe you've already tried to meditate, only to find your mind running laps around your to-do list. Or perhaps you've attempted to embrace impermanence, but the thought of letting go of certain attachments feels, well… impossible.

So, as we wrap up this chapter, take a breath. Notice where you are right now—what you're feeling, what thoughts are passing through. And remember, wherever you are on this journey, you're doing just fine. There's no rush, no finish line, no perfect version of you waiting at the end. There's only this moment, this breath, and the gentle, ongoing practice of being here.

Let's keep going, together.

Chapter 13:
Overcoming Challenges in Buddhist Practice

You've made the decision to explore Buddhist principles and integrate them into your life—maybe it's meditation, mindful breathing, or simply trying to be more present in your day. But even with the best intentions, practice can sometimes feel... messy. You sit down to meditate and your mind won't stop racing. You try to be mindful, but then someone cuts you off in traffic and—bam—there goes your patience.

If you're nodding along, you're not alone. One of the most beautiful (and, let's be real, most frustrating) truths about Buddhism is that it's a practice. It's not about reaching perfection or instantly changing your life into a serene oasis. It's about the daily, imperfect attempts to bring a little more peace, awareness, and compassion into your world—even when it feels like everything's working against you.

This chapter is your gentle guide through the common challenges that arise in Buddhist practice—from restless minds to feelings of "I'm doing this wrong." We'll explore why these hurdles are normal, how they're actually a part of the path, and, most importantly, how to handle them with kindness toward yourself. You'll discover practical tips and habits to keep going when things get tough and learn why these very challenges are the doorway to deeper growth.

Remember, there's no one right way to practice Buddhism. It's deeply personal, evolving, and full of trial and error. The key is consistency and patience, with a good dose of self-compassion along the way. Let's dive into how you can keep moving forward, even when the path feels bumpy.

Overcoming Spiritual Fatigue

Despite your best efforts, there might come a moment when your Buddhist practice starts to feel heavy. What once brought peace now feels like another item on your to-do list. Meditation feels like a chore, mindfulness slips through your fingers, and you find yourself wondering, *Is this even helping anymore?*

Welcome to spiritual fatigue—and trust me, it's more common than you think. Burnout doesn't just happen in work or relationships; it can sneak into your spiritual life, too. And it doesn't mean you're failing. It just means it's time to pause, reflect, and gently reset.

Exercise: Recognizing Burnout in Your Practice

Let's start by identifying if you're experiencing spiritual fatigue. Grab a journal or simply sit quietly for a few moments. Take a few deep breaths and ask yourself:

- **"How do I feel before, during, and after my practice?"**

  - Are you excited or do you feel dread?

  - Do you feel calmer afterward or more frustrated?

- **"Why did I begin this practice?"**

  - Has that intention changed?

  - Are you focusing more on "doing it right" than on how it makes you feel?

- **"Am I being too rigid with myself?"**

  - Are your expectations around your practice too high?

  - Are you allowing space for flexibility and imperfection?

If your answers reveal frustration, dread, or a sense of obligation rather than connection, you're likely experiencing spiritual fatigue. And that's okay; it's simply your mind and heart's way of asking for a little care.

Exercise: Reinvigorating Your Practice

Now, let's breathe some fresh energy back into your practice:

- **Reset your "why":** Close your eyes and think back to why you started this journey. Was it for peace? Clarity? Compassion? Picture that intention as a soft light within you. Allow it to grow and fill you with warmth. This is your anchor, the core of why you practice.

- **Simplify, simplify, simplify:** Spiritual fatigue often comes when we overcomplicate things. For the next week, strip your practice down to its essence. Maybe that means meditating for just three minutes instead of twenty, or focusing on one deep breath before starting your day. Small steps can bring powerful shifts.

- **Reintroduce joy:** Think about which parts of your practice bring you genuine joy—is it walking meditation, chanting, or simply sitting in nature? Prioritize these. Joy is a powerful motivator, and when your practice feels light and fulfilling, you're more likely to stick with it.

- **Practice self-compassion:** Every time you feel that heaviness creeping back in, gently remind yourself: "It's okay. I'm human. This is part of the journey." Imagine you're speaking to your best friend and offer yourself that same kindness.

Spiritual fatigue isn't a sign that you've failed; it's an invitation to soften, reassess, and find new ways to connect. Your practice doesn't have to be perfect or profound every single day. Some days, just showing up—even imperfectly—is more than enough. And sometimes, stepping back and resting is the most spiritual thing you can do.

The Power of Patience

If there's one thing Buddhist practice teaches us (over and over again), it's this: Growth doesn't happen overnight. It's slow, subtle, and often invisible until, suddenly, it's not. But waiting for that change can be frustrating. You meditate daily, practice mindfulness, and still find yourself losing your temper or feeling anxious. You might start wondering, *Why isn't this working yet?*

Buddhist practice can be compared to planting a seed. You water it, give it sunlight, and care for it daily, but you don't yank it out of the ground every week to see if it's grown. You trust the process, even when you can't see the results. That's where patience comes in—not just waiting passively, but actively trusting that every small effort is creating change beneath the surface.

Exercise: Cultivating Patience and Building Perseverance

Let's walk through a practice to help you build patience and see the value in slow, steady growth.

Reflect on your personal growth journey:

1. Find a place where you won't be disturbed and sit comfortably. Close your eyes and take a few deep, cleansing breaths.

2. Think back to one area of your life where you've grown over time—something that didn't happen overnight. It could be learning a skill, healing from a tough experience, or even becoming more compassionate.

3. Ask yourself:

   ○ "What small steps led to that growth?"

   ○ "Were there moments when I felt stuck or frustrated?"

   ○ "How do I feel now compared to when I started?"

This reflection helps you see that gradual change has already happened in your life—it's just easy to forget in the moment.

Create a Patience Anchor

1. Choose a simple daily action in your Buddhist practice, like focusing on your breath for one minute or noticing one mindful moment in your day. This will be your "patience anchor"—a reminder that small, consistent steps matter.

2. Every time you complete this action, say to yourself: "This is enough. I am growing, even if I can't see it yet."

This practice rewires your mind to celebrate small efforts, building perseverance over time.

Practice the Pause and Breathe Technique

1. The next time you feel impatient, whether during meditation or in daily life, pause for just a moment.

2. Take three slow, deep breaths.

3. As you breathe, silently repeat: "I am exactly where I need to be. Growth takes time."

This simple technique creates space between your frustration and your response, helping you practice patience in real time.

Patience isn't about passively waiting; it's about actively trusting that the small, sometimes invisible efforts you're making are shaping you in ways you can't always see. Buddhist practice is a lifelong journey, and every breath, every mindful moment, is part of that path. Perseverance is what keeps you moving forward, even when progress feels slow. And in that steady, patient commitment, true transformation happens.

Trusting the Process

One of the trickiest parts of Buddhist practice? Trusting the process—especially when things get hard or when progress feels nonexistent. You might find yourself wondering, *Am I even doing this right?* or *Why am I not feeling more peaceful by now?*

This is where *saddhā*—faith or trust in the path — becomes essential. But let's be clear: In Buddhism, faith isn't about blind belief. It's about confidence grounded in experience—the kind of trust that says, "Even if I can't see the results yet, I believe this path is leading me somewhere meaningful."

When you're planting that garden, you water the seeds even before they sprout, because you trust the process. You might not see growth today, or even tomorrow, but you keep tending the soil because you know something is happening beneath the surface. Your practice works the same way.

But staying motivated when there's no obvious progress? That's tough. So, let's walk through how to build that trust, even when things get difficult.

Exercise: Recognizing the Need for Motivation and Cultivating Trust

Notice where you're feeling stuck:
1. Sit comfortably, close your eyes, and take a few deep breaths.

2. Think about one area of your Buddhist practice or life where you feel stuck or unmotivated. Maybe it's your meditation routine, your efforts to practice mindfulness, or simply managing daily stress.

3. Ask yourself:

   ○ "What's making this feel hard?"

   ○ "Am I expecting quick results?"

   ○ "Do I feel disconnected from my original intention?"

Sometimes, just acknowledging where you're struggling can bring a bit of clarity and soften that inner critic.

Reconnect With Moments of Progress

1. Now, think back to any small wins you've had—even the tiniest moments. Maybe you handled a frustrating situation with more patience than usual, or you noticed your breath before reacting impulsively.

2. Write down three small signs that your practice is making a difference. They don't need to be groundbreaking. Something like "I felt a little calmer after my morning meditation" counts.

These small moments are proof that your practice is working, even if the bigger changes are still unfolding.

Create a "Trust the Process" Reminder

1. Choose a simple phrase or mantra that resonates with you, like:

   ○ "Every breath counts."

- "Growth is happening, even if I can't see it."

- "I trust the process."

2. Write it on a sticky note, set it as your phone wallpaper, or say it silently during meditation.

3. Whenever you feel your motivation dip, return to this reminder. It's your gentle nudge back to trust.

Practice Appreciation for the Path

1. At the end of your day, take two minutes to reflect on your practice, no judgment allowed.

2. Ask yourself:

   - "Which part of my practice brought me even a moment of peace or clarity today?"

   - "What am I grateful for in this journey, even if it's challenging?"

Appreciating the path—even in its messy moments—helps build that deep, lasting trust.

Here's the heart of it: Trusting the process isn't about feeling zen 24/7 or nailing every meditation session. It's about showing up, even when you're not sure it's working, and having faith that each moment of practice—each breath, each pause, each act of mindfulness—is leading you somewhere meaningful.

It's okay to feel unmotivated sometimes. It's okay to question things. But underneath it all, remember this: Growth is happening, even when you can't see it. And that trust? That's what will keep you going, one mindful breath at a time.

Celebrating the Wins

When you're deep in your practice—whether it's meditating daily, being more mindful, or simply trying to be more compassionate—it's easy to get caught up in what's not going right. Maybe you missed a few meditation sessions this week, lost your patience with someone, or got distracted halfway through your breathing practice. Suddenly, you're focusing only on the failures and completely overlooking the moments when you did show up.

In Buddhism, the journey itself is just as important as the destination. Every mindful breath, every time you choose kindness, every moment you notice your thoughts instead of being swept away by them—that's progress. It's easy to overlook these moments because they seem so small, but they're the building blocks of real, lasting change.

Celebrating your wins not only acknowledges how far you've come but also keeps you motivated. It fosters gratitude for the journey, even when it feels slow or challenging. And recognizing these moments actually helps deepen your practice.

Exercise: Tracking Progress and Celebrating Wins

Let's create a simple but powerful way to start seeing and celebrating your growth.

Create a Mindful Wins Journal

1. Grab a notebook, or use the notes app on your phone—whatever works best for you.

2. Label it "Mindful Wins" or something that feels right. This will be your space to track even the smallest signs of progress.

Daily Reflection (Five Minutes a Day)

At the end of each day, take five minutes to reflect and write down:

- **One mindful moment:**

    o   Did you pause before reacting?

    o   Did you notice your breath without trying?

    o   Did you choose compassion over frustration?

    o   Even a moment of awareness counts.

- **One challenge you faced:**

    o   Maybe you lost your temper, felt distracted during meditation, or struggled with impatience.

    o   This isn't about judging yourself, just acknowledging where things felt tough.

- **One thing you're grateful for in your practice:**

    o   It could be something simple, like "I felt a bit calmer today" or "I remembered to breathe before responding to that stressful email."

This daily reflection helps you balance the hard moments with the good, cultivating gratitude and awareness of your growth.

Weekly Celebration Check-In

At the end of the week, review your journal entries and ask yourself:

- "What patterns do I see?"

- Are there moments that keep showing up? Like feeling more patient, having more mindful mornings, or reacting with less frustration?

- "What progress am I proud of?"

  - It could be something big, like sticking to your meditation routine, or something small, like simply being more aware of your thoughts.

Now, celebrate it:

- Treat yourself to something simple—a favorite cup of tea, a peaceful walk in nature, or even just taking a few extra minutes to relax.

- As you do so, silently acknowledge: "This is for me. I'm growing, step by step."

Share Your Wins (If It Feels Right)

Sometimes, sharing your progress can amplify your sense of accomplishment. If you have a friend, community, or meditation group, share your small wins. You might say, "This week, I noticed I was kinder to myself," or "I finally managed to meditate five days in a row!"

If you prefer to keep it private, that's perfectly fine—just make sure you recognize it.

Growth isn't always obvious. It often happens in tiny, almost invisible steps. But those steps add up. By celebrating your wins—regardless of their size—you're reinforcing your commitment, building gratitude, and making your practice something that brings joy, not just discipline.

So, give yourself permission to be proud. You're doing the work. And that, in itself, is a win worth celebrating.

Final Thoughts

You've made it through some of the most meaningful and sometimes messy parts of Buddhist practice—from managing challenges and overcoming spiritual fatigue to creating patience, trusting the process, and, most importantly, celebrating your wins. And here you are, still showing up. That in itself is something worth acknowledging.

But now comes the exciting part: putting it all together.

In the next chapter, we'll take everything you've learned and turn it into a simple, empowering road map. No rigid schedules or overwhelming commitments. You'll create a practice that fits you and your life. One that feels natural, supportive, and sustainable.

So, as you prepare to step into this next chapter, acknowledge how far you've come. And remember: There's no perfect way to walk this path. There's only your way—one mindful breath, one small step at a time.

Let's dive into this final part of the journey together.

Chapter 14:
A Four-Week Practice Plan—Integrating Buddhism Into Your Life

Think of this chapter as your personal guide to creating a simple, meaningful, and totally doable four-week Buddhist-inspired practice plan. No, this isn't a one-size-fits-all program, and it's definitely not about following some rigid set of rules. Throughout these chapters, you've learned that Buddhism isn't about that. It's about finding what resonates with you—what feels right in your mind, body, and heart.

This chapter will help you take the insights and practices you've learned and blend them into your daily routine in a way that feels natural. We'll look at small, realistic steps that, over four weeks, can make a big impact. The idea is to help you build consistency, create habits that stick, and, most importantly, develop a practice that feels personal and sustainable.

Whether you're aiming to create more mindfulness, reduce stress, or simply feel more connected to yourself and others, this plan is here to guide you—without overwhelming you. We'll focus on achievable daily practices, small reflections, and habits that offer both immediate moments of peace and long-term, life-changing effects.

And here's the best part: You get to customize it. This chapter isn't about telling you the right way—it's about helping you create it your way.

So, are you ready to start building your four-week practice plan? Let's dive in.

WEEK ONE: Building the Foundation

Welcome to week one! This is where we start planting the seeds for your four-week practice. The focus this week is on three key Buddhist concepts: *dukkha* (the inevitable challenges, dissatisfaction, and suffering that life brings), *samudaya* (the truth behind our cravings), and *nirodha* (the freedom that comes when we learn to let go of our cravings and attachments).

Think of this week as a gentle yet powerful invitation to look at where you're holding on too tightly—whether it's to expectations, emotions, habits, or even people—and how that might be contributing to stress or unhappiness. No need to force anything. Just bring awareness, curiosity, and compassion to whatever comes up.

Here's how week one will flow.

Morning Practice: Journaling About Current Challenges and Sources of Craving (5–10 Minutes)

Start your day by setting aside a few quiet moments for journaling. Reflect on:

- What's challenging you right now?

- Where do you notice stress, dissatisfaction, or frustration?

- Are there any cravings or attachments fueling those feelings (wanting things to be different, chasing perfection, needing external validation, etc.)?

This isn't about judging yourself or labeling things as good or bad. It's about gently shining a light on what's there. Over the week, you might start noticing patterns—certain cravings or attachments that keep showing up. That's valuable insight.

Prompt ideas:

- What's causing me the most stress today?

- Where am I holding on too tightly?

- Is there something I'm craving that's pulling me away from the present moment?

Evening Reflection: A Five-Minute Meditation on Impermanence

As the day winds down, practice a simple meditation that focuses on *anicca*—the Buddhist teaching of impermanence. Everything changes: emotions, thoughts, situations, and even this very moment.

Here's how:

1. Sit comfortably, close your eyes, and take a few deep breaths.

2. Bring awareness to your breath, noticing its natural rise and fall.

3. Reflect on something from your day that felt challenging or intense.

4. Gently remind yourself: "This too is impermanent." Notice how the feeling or thought shifts as you hold it with kindness and nonjudgment.

This practice helps you connect with the truth that nothing is fixed—not your emotions, struggles, or cravings. Things pass. Knowing this can bring a deep sense of peace.

Daily Exercise: Identify One Craving or Attachment to Release

Throughout your day, bring awareness to moments when cravings or attachments pop up. These can be big or small:

- reaching for your phone when you're bored

- craving praise for a job well done

- wanting someone to react a certain way

When you notice a craving, pause. Ask yourself:
- "Is this serving me right now?"

- "Can I gently let this go?"

You don't have to let go perfectly. Even just noticing the craving and pausing before acting on it is a huge step. Over time, this builds your ability to release attachments that no longer serve you.

Tip: At the end of each day, jot down in your journal:

- What craving or attachment did I notice today?

- Was I able to release it? How did that feel?

By the end of week one, you'll likely notice a shift in how you relate to challenges and cravings. The simple act of observing—without judgment—creates space between you and your reactions. That space is where freedom lives.

Remember: This practice isn't about becoming perfect or eliminating desires altogether. It's about understanding the role they play and gently learning how to let go when they cause unnecessary suffering.

One breath, one craving, one release at a time.

WEEK TWO: Transforming Perception

Welcome to week two! After spending the first week exploring life's challenges and practicing the art of letting go, we now shift our focus inward to how we perceive the world and how our intentions shape our actions. This week is all about seeing with greater clarity and purpose—foundational elements in Buddhism known as Right View and Right Intention, the first two steps of the Eightfold Path.

Our perceptions influence everything—how we react, how we connect, and even how we suffer. When we view the world through the lens of fear, judgment, or ego, it can cloud our experience. But when we approach life with clarity, compassion, and purposeful intention, everything softens, even the challenges.

This week, you'll practice setting clear, compassionate intentions and notice how your thoughts and perceptions shape your experience. The goal isn't to "get it right" but to become more aware of your mind's filters and gently begin to transform them.

Here's how week two will flow.

Morning Practice: Setting an Intention Aligned With Compassion and Purpose (5–10 Minutes)

Start your mornings by setting an intention that guides your day with clarity and compassion. Intentions aren't rigid goals or tasks—they're gentle reminders that help ground you in how you want to *be* in the world. Get started as follows:

1. Sit quietly for a few moments, focusing on your breath.

2. Reflect on how you want to approach the day. Ask yourself:

   o "How can I bring more compassion into my interactions today?"

   o "What's one way I can align my actions with my deeper purpose?"

3. Choose an intention that feels meaningful. For example:

   o "Today, I will listen deeply and without judgment."

- ○ "I will approach challenges with patience and kindness."

- ○ "I will recognize the humanity in everyone I encounter."

Write your intention in your journal or on a sticky note to keep it top of mind throughout the day.

Mindful Moments: Pausing to Reflect on Perception

Throughout the day, practice small pauses to check in on how your perceptions are shaping your experiences. Perceptions can be tricky—they're often influenced by past experiences, assumptions, or mood.

When to pause:

- during a moment of frustration (traffic, an annoying email, etc.)

- when you're feeling particularly joyful or peaceful

- in moments of interaction—especially when you feel judged or misunderstood

Ask yourself:

- "Is what I'm seeing the full picture?"

- "Am I reacting based on an assumption or a deeper truth?"

- "Can I see this situation (or person) with more compassion?"

The goal isn't to stop your thoughts but to simply *notice* them and how they color your view of reality. Even a few mindful pauses each day can shift how you experience the world.

Evening Reflection: Writing About One Moment of Clarity (5–10 Minutes)

At the end of your day, spend a few moments reflecting on your experiences, especially focusing on any moments where you felt you saw things more clearly.

Use these journal prompts:

- Was there a moment today when I noticed my perception shift?

- Did I catch myself reacting based on assumptions?

- How did setting an intention this morning impact my choices today?

- Was there a moment when I saw a person or situation with more compassion or understanding?

This reflection helps reinforce moments when you were able to step back and see things as they are—without the usual filters or judgments. Over time, these moments grow, leading to a deeper sense of clarity and peace.

By the end of week two, you'll start noticing how much your perceptions influence your daily life—not in a self-critical way, but with curiosity and kindness. Understanding the mind's filters and choosing to see through a lens of compassion creates powerful shifts.

And setting intentions? It plants the seeds for meaningful change. Each day becomes an opportunity to align your thoughts and actions with your deeper values.

This week is about embracing the idea that we can't always change what happens, but we *can* transform how we see and respond to it.

One intention, one mindful moment, one clear perception at a time.

WEEK THREE: Mindful Communication and Living

Welcome to week three! You've spent the last two weeks exploring how challenges, cravings, perceptions, and intentions shape your experience. Now, it's time to bring that awareness into how you *show up* in the world—through your words, your actions, and the way you live your life.

This week focuses on three powerful aspects of the Buddhist Eightfold Path: Right Speech, Right Action, and Right Livelihood. These aren't about living a perfect, saintly life but making small, conscious choices that reflect your deepest values. It's about communicating with kindness, acting with integrity, and living in a way that feels aligned with who you truly are.

The practices this week will help you build mindfulness into your daily interactions, turning conversations, choices, and even work into opportunities for deeper awareness and compassion.

Here's how week three will flow.

Morning Practice: Recite a Personal Mantra to Guide Your Speech and Actions (3–5 Minutes)

Begin your day by grounding yourself with a simple, meaningful mantra that sets the tone for how you want to communicate and act. Mantras help create a gentle reminder to pause and choose mindfulness throughout the day, especially during challenging moments. Begin by doing the following:

1. Sit quietly, focusing on your breath.

2. Reflect on how you want to speak and act today. Consider:

    o "How can I communicate with kindness and truth?"

    o "How can I make choices that align with my values?"

3. Create a mantra that feels right for you. Examples:

    ○ "I speak with compassion and truth."

    ○ "My actions reflect my deepest values."

    ○ "I live mindfully, with kindness and integrity."

Repeat your mantra three times, either aloud or silently, letting it sink in. Return to it during the day whenever you need a grounding reminder.

Daily Challenge: Practice Kind, Truthful, and Necessary Speech

Words carry immense power—they can heal, hurt, connect, or divide. This week, the challenge is to practice Right Speech, which means aiming for communication that's kind, truthful, and necessary.

Throughout your day, pause before speaking and ask yourself:

• "Is what I'm about to say true?"

• "Is it kind?"

• "Is it necessary?"

This doesn't mean sugarcoating your thoughts or avoiding honesty—it means being mindful about how you express yourself. Even difficult conversations can be approached with compassion and respect.

Bonus challenge: Notice moments when silence might be more powerful than words. Sometimes, the kindest, most mindful choice is to simply listen.

Evening Reflection: Writing About Aligned Actions (5–10 Minutes)

End your day by reflecting on how your words and actions aligned with your values. This practice helps reinforce mindful communication and behavior while offering insight into areas for growth.

Try these journal prompts:

- Was there a moment today when I spoke with kindness and honesty? How did that feel?

- Did I catch myself speaking out of habit, judgment, or frustration? What triggered that?

- Was there a situation where I acted in alignment with my deeper values?

- How did my interactions today reflect (or not reflect) the person I want to be?

This isn't about judging yourself—it's about noticing patterns and celebrating moments when you lived in alignment with your intentions.

Mindful communication and living are at the heart of a meaningful Buddhist practice. By becoming more aware of how you speak, act, and live, you naturally create more harmony within yourself and in your relationships.

The beauty of this week's focus is that it turns everyday moments—conversations with friends, emails to coworkers, even small talk with strangers—into opportunities for growth and compassion. It also invites you to reflect on Right Livelihood—whether the way you earn a living or spend your time supports your values and contributes positively to the world.

No need for drastic life changes here—this is about small, intentional shifts that bring more authenticity and kindness into your daily life.

One word, one action, one mindful choice at a time.

WEEK FOUR: Deepening Awareness and Letting Go

Welcome to week four—the final week of your journey! This week is all about deepening your awareness, refining your mindfulness, and exploring the profound Buddhist teaching of *anatta*—the concept of no-self.

Over the past three weeks, you've built a strong foundation by understanding life's challenges, transforming your perceptions, and practicing mindful communication and living. Now, it's time to bring it all together, cultivating a deeper sense of presence and learning how to let go of ego and judgment, two things that often stand between us and inner peace.

We'll focus on Right Effort (gently guiding your energy toward growth), Right Mindfulness (being fully present), Right Concentration (deepening focus), and *anatta* (loosening our grip on the ego).

This week invites you to settle into stillness, observe with curiosity, and celebrate how far you've come.

Here's how week four will flow.

Morning Practice: 10-Minute Mindfulness Meditation Focusing on the Breath

Start your mornings by grounding yourself in the simple, yet powerful, practice of mindful breathing. This strengthens Right Mindfulness and Right Concentration, helping you approach the day with calm awareness.

Here's how to practice:

1. Get cozy in a place you won't be disturbed. Close your eyes or lower your gaze.

2. Take a few deep breaths, inhaling through the nose and exhaling through the mouth.

3. Let your breath settle into its natural rhythm.

4. Focus your attention on the sensation of your breath—the rise and fall of your chest, the feeling of air moving through your nostrils.

5. When your mind wanders (and it will), gently guide your attention back to the breath without judgment.

This practice isn't about clearing the mind but about noticing where your attention goes and lovingly bringing it back to the present moment. Over time, this builds mental clarity and calm.

Midday Practice: Mindfulness Walk or Mindful Eating Exercise

Incorporate mindfulness into your daily routine through simple activities like walking or eating. These practices ground you in the present moment and cultivate Right Effort—the gentle, sustained focus on being here, now.

Mindfulness Walk

1. Step outside, even if it's just around your neighborhood or yard.

2. Walk slowly, paying attention to each step. Notice how your feet feel against the ground, the rhythm of your breath, and the sounds around you.

3. Let thoughts come and go without clinging to them. If your mind wanders, return to the sensation of walking.

Mindful Eating

1. Choose one meal or snack to eat mindfully.

2. Before eating, pause and observe the food—its colors, textures, and aromas.

3. Take small bites, chewing slowly and fully tasting each bite. Notice the flavors, textures, and how your body feels as you eat.

4. Avoid distractions (no phones, TV, or multitasking) and simply be present with the act of eating.

Evening Reflection: Writing About Letting Go of Ego or Judgment (5–10 Minutes)

End each day by reflecting on moments when you were able to let go of something—whether it was a judgmental thought, the need to be right, or even a moment of self-doubt. This practice helps you explore the concept of *anatta*, gently loosening your grip on the ego.

Use these journal prompts:

- Was there a moment today when I caught myself judging someone (or myself) and was able to let that go?

- Did I notice my ego taking control today? How did that feel?

- Was there a situation where I was able to step back and simply observe without attaching to a specific identity or outcome?

- How did letting go (even for a moment) shift my experience?

This reflection isn't about shaming yourself for ego-driven moments—it's about gently noticing them and celebrating when you were able to release them, even briefly.

Final Day: Reflect, Celebrate, and Set New Intentions

You made it! The final day is all about pausing to reflect on your journey, celebrating your growth, and setting intentions for how you want to continue integrating Buddhist practices into your life.

Reflection Questions

- What shifts have I noticed in myself over the past four weeks?

- Which practices resonated most deeply with me?

- Where did I experience the most growth?

- What was the biggest challenge, and what did it teach me?

- How has my relationship with mindfulness, compassion, or letting go changed?

Celebration and Intention-Setting

- Write a letter to yourself, acknowledging the effort and commitment you've made.

- Celebrate your progress—whether that means treating yourself to something special, sharing your experience with a friend, or simply taking a moment of gratitude.

- Set one or two gentle intentions for how you'll continue this journey moving forward. These could be as simple as:

    o "I will continue my morning meditation three times a week."

    o "I will bring mindful awareness to my meals."

o "I will practice kind and truthful speech daily."

Remember: This isn't the end—it's just the beginning of an ongoing personal journey.

Deepening awareness and letting go of ego is the heart of Buddhist practice. It allows you to move through life with more freedom, less stress, and a greater sense of connection to yourself and the world.

The practices from this week, and the entire four-week journey, are centered around progress, patience, and presence.

You've built a strong foundation, and now you have the tools to continue growing in a way that feels authentic and meaningful to you.

One breath, one moment, one release at a time.

Finish this journey strong, present, and open to what comes next.

Conclusion:
Your Path Forward

As we come to the end of this journey together, I hope you feel a little more grounded, a bit more at ease, and perhaps even inspired to explore your own path with Buddhism. This book wasn't about mastering every principle or practice perfectly—it was about opening a door. A door to 12 life-changing Buddhist practices that can help reduce stress, clear your mind, and guide you toward inner peace, even amid the challenges of today's world.

Through these pages, we explored what it means to understand life's challenges, recognizing that suffering is an inherent part of the human experience. But rather than viewing that as a burden, Buddhism teaches us that embracing this truth creates space for healing and deeper connection. You also learned the power of letting go—of attachments, expectations, and the stories we sometimes cling to. In that release, we find the kind of freedom that lightens both mind and heart.

We talked about cultivating a positive mindset, where gratitude and compassion reshape how we see ourselves and the world. And of course, we explored mindfulness—the practice of simply being present, here and now, turning everyday moments into opportunities for clarity, connection, and peace.

The most important takeaway? This journey is yours. There's no one way to practice Buddhism. No gold stars or checkboxes. It's deeply personal, ever-evolving, and built on patience and consistency. Even the smallest steps—taking a mindful breath, expressing gratitude, or pausing before reacting—can ripple into profound changes over time.

So, as you close this book and step back into your day, I encourage you to pick just one practice that resonated with you. Start small. Let it grow naturally, without pressure or perfection. Remember, the path is the practice.

If this book offered you even a glimpse of peace, clarity, or inspiration, I'd be incredibly grateful if you could share your thoughts through a review. Your feedback not only helps others find this guide but also supports me in continuing to create meaningful work.

Thank you for allowing me to walk alongside you on this first step of your journey. May you find ease in your challenges, joy in your moments, and peace within yourself.

With gratitude and mindfulness.

References

Aske, J. (2019, March 2). *Kindness by John Aske*. Buddhism Now. https://buddhismnow.com/2019/03/02/kindness-by-john-aske/

Babauta, L. (n.d.). *The Zen habits guide to letting go of attachments*. Zen Habits. https://zenhabits.net/attachments/

Bjarnadottir, A., & Amjera, R. (2023, January 4). *Mindful eating 101 — A beginner's guide*. Healthline. https://www.healthline.com/nutrition/mindful-eating-guide

The Buddha and his teachings – OCR. (n.d.). BBC Bitesize. https://www.bbc.co.uk/bitesize/guides/zj4g4qt/revision/4

De Ridder, Y. (n.d.). *7 tips for positive thinking to shift your mindset*. Loving Life Today. https://www.lovinglifetoday.com/tips-for-positive-thinking/

Djernis, D., Lerstrup, I., Poulsen, D., Stigsdotter, U., Dahlgaard, J., & O'Toole, M. (2019). A systematic review and meta-analysis of nature-based mindfulness: Effects of moving mindfulness training into an outdoor natural setting. *International Journal of Environmental Research and Public Health*, *16*(17), 3202. https://doi.org/10.3390/ijerph16173202

Fischer, N. (2024, August 14). *Impermanence is Buddha nature*. Lion's Roar. https://www.lionsroar.com/impermanence-is-buddha-nature/

The 5 precepts: Buddhism and morality. (2019, January 30). Buddho.org. https://buddho.org/buddhism-and-morality-the-five-precepts/

The four noble truths: Essence of the dhamma. (2022, December 25). Buddho.org. https://buddho.org/buddhism/

Fryburg, D. A. (2021). Kindness as a stress reduction–health promotion intervention: A review of the psychobiology of caring. *American Journal of Lifestyle Medicine, 16*(1), 89–100. https://doi.org/10.1177/1559827620988268

The Healthline Editorial Team. (2020, March 29). *Causes of stress: Recognizing and managing your stressors.* Healthline. https://www.healthline.com/health/stress-causes

Henwood, D. (2022, September 7). *Why the Old English concept of kindness holds the key to effective business communication.* LinkedIn. https://www.linkedin.com/pulse/why-old-english-concept-kindness-holds-key-effective-henwood-phd

History.com Editors. (2024, April 5). *Buddhism.* History. https://www.history.com/topics/religion/buddhism

Huxter, M. (n.d.-a). Dukkha: The Buddhist philosophy of suffering. *Insight Timer Blog.* https://insighttimer.com/blog/dukkha-meaning-buddhism/

Huxter, M. (n.d.-b). How Buddhist's approach mindfulness and meditation. *Insight Timer Blog.* https://insighttimer.com/blog/mindfulness-in-buddhism-secular-meditation/

Kadampa, L. (2018, February 19). *Love, attachment, and desire in Buddhism.* Medium. https://medium.com/@lunakadampa/love-attachment-and-desire-in-buddhism-983c97980fad

Lama Karma Yeshe Chödrön. (2023, March 30). *The eightfold path: Right effort.* Lion's Roar. https://www.lionsroar.com/right-effort/

Morin, A. (2023, April 17). *How to know if Zen meditation is right for you.* Verywell Mind. https://www.verywellmind.com/what-is-zen-meditation-4586721

No self (anatta). (n.d.). Lion's Roar. https://www.lionsroar.com/buddhism/no-self-anatta/

The noble eightfold path. (n.d.). *Namchak Tibetan Buddhist Practice & Retreat*. https://www.namchak.org/community/blog/the-noble-eightfold-path/

Oakes, S. (2018, June 1). *The four noble truths*. Spirit Rock. https://www.spiritrock.org/practice-guides/the-four-noble-truths

Order of Engaged Buddhists. (2014, January 11). *Contemplative practice*. https://orderengagedbuddhists.com/contemplative-practice/

Pendall, J. L. (2018, February 7). *What is right intention, anyway? {The eightfold path}*. The Tattooed Buddha. https://thetattooedbuddha.com/2018/02/07/what-is-right-intention-anyway-the-eightfold-path/

Peto, A. (2022, March 20). *Practicing Buddhism during challenging and difficult times*. Alan Peto. https://alanpeto.com/buddhism/buddhism-hard-times/

Qiao-Tasserit, E., Garcia Quesada, M., Antico, L., Bavelier, D., Vuilleumier, P., & Pichon, S. (2017). Transient emotional events and individual affective traits affect emotion recognition in a perceptual decision-making task. *PLOS One, 12*(2), e0171375. https://doi.org/10.1371/journal.pone.0171375

Resolving conflicts as Buddhists. (2022, July 17). World Tribune. https://www.worldtribune.org/2022/resolving-conflicts-as-buddhists/

Right effort, right mindfulness, and right concentration (mental discipline). (2024, July 22). Fiveable.me. https://library.fiveable.me/introduction-buddhism/unit-3/effort-mindfulness-concentration-mental-discipline/study-guide/7bZEHVvCA2lhv2XK

Rinzler, L. (2023, September 15). *Making your work matter: A Buddhist view on finding your career.* Medium. https://lodrorinzler.medium.com/making-your-work-matter-a-buddhist-view-on-finding-your-633e3e3517b8

SingleCare Team. (2024, November 4). Stress statistics: How common is stress, and who's most affected? *The Checkup.* https://www.singlecare.com/blog/news/stress-statistics/

Tabac, M. (2021, October 11). *The neuroscience of journaling and its benefits.* Medium. https://medium.com/clear-yo-mind/the-neuroscience-of-journaling-and-its-benefits-a91218773159

TMP Admin. (2016, October 21). Mindful nature connection. *The Mindfulness Project.* https://web.archive.org/web/20240610024443/https://www.londonmindful.com/about-the-project

Travers, M. (2024, May 27). 3 reasons we keep replaying conversations in our heads. *Psychology Today.* https://www.psychologytoday.com/ca/blog/social-instincts/202405/3-reasons-why-we-replay-conversations-in-our-minds

Uijterwaal, D. (2021, June 12). *The importance of accepting suffering, pain, fear, and trauma in your life.* Medium. https://medium.com/change-your-mind/the-importance-of-accepting-suffering-pain-fear-and-trauma-in-your-life-a2e641925e07

Veritas. (2021, June 25). *What does right action mean?* Medium. https://medium.com/new-earth-consciousness/what-does-right-action-mean-ed853d39c9ee

Made in United States
Orlando, FL
17 June 2025

62187483R00095